MENTORING FOR MISSION

Mentoring for Mission

Nurturing New Faculty
at Church-Related Colleges

Caroline J. Simon
Laura Bloxham
Denise Doyle
Mel Hailey
Jane Hokanson Hawks
Kathleen Light
Dominic P. Scibilia
Ernest Simmons

WILLIAM B. EERDMANS PUBLISHING COMPANY
GRAND RAPIDS, MICHIGAN / CAMBRIDGE, U.K.

© 2003 Wm. B. Eerdmans Publishing Co.
All rights reserved

Wm. B. Eerdmans Publishing Co.
255 Jefferson Ave. S.E., Grand Rapids, Michigan 49503 /
P.O. Box 163, Cambridge CB3 9PU U.K.

Printed in the United States of America

08 07 06 05 04 03   7 6 5 4 3 2 1

Library of Congress Cataloging-in-Publication Data

ISBN 0-8028-2124-3

www.eerdmans.com

For Arlin G. Meyer,

in gratitude for his many years of service
to the Lilly Fellows Program in Humanities and the Arts
and to the Lilly Network of Colleges and Universities

Contents

Contents

Mentoring as an Exercise of Practical Wisdom

- *What Makes This Book Unique*
- *Why We Couldn't Write "Mentoring for Dummies"*
- *How to Use This Book*

What Makes This Book Unique

Welcome, care, and concern for others should be hallmarks of Christian communities. Yet Shelly Cunningham, in her 1999 study of workplace mentoring at Christian colleges, found that although 93 percent of surveyed faculty thought that senior faculty have a responsibility to mentor new faculty, only a small minority reported having served as a mentor to another faculty member. Among the hindrances to mentoring noted by the study participants were heavy teaching loads and large classes that squeeze out time for mentoring. Most significantly, among the reasons given for the lack of mentoring at the surveyed institutions were "no institutional value placed on mentoring" and "no intentional development or formal training programs for new faculty."

Unless a college institutionalizes its commitment to becoming a mentoring community, overworked faculty are unlikely to make time either to be mentors or to be mentored. Assuming that mentoring will "just happen" may leave those who need it most without a resource that could help them be more effective teachers and scholars. New college faculty members are too valuable to allow their development to occur haphazardly.

Well-designed mentoring programs lead to more confident junior faculty members who understand their home institutions and enthusiastically contribute to institutional mission. Moreover, a mentoring relationship that has nothing to do with merit raises, reappointment, tenure, and promotion has many benefits. Chairpersons, deans, and provosts have their own responsibilities in nurturing new faculty, and they may also design and implement faculty development programs. But, as an addition to mentoring done through administrative channels, faculty-centered mentoring helps create a climate in which new faculty can express their real concerns, reveal their felt inadequacies, and voice their puzzlements and observations about the effect of the founding tradition of the institution on the educational enterprise. Facilitated mentoring programs that are faculty-centered and independent of supervisory lines can provide a "safe space" for new faculty to talk about how they see themselves and where their "growing edge" is vis-à-vis the mission of the college or university.

> *The identity of an institution lies, not in what anyone says about it from time to time, but in what everyone does about it every day.*
>
> — Jeanne Knoerle, in "The Love of Learning and the Desire for God," 19

Though some of what we have to tell you would apply to nurturing new faculty in any institution of higher learning, our focus will be on mentoring in the context of church-related colleges and universities: mentoring for Christian mission. We see mentoring in a Christian context not just as a means of achieving institutional goals but also as an expression of the Christian virtues, especially practical wisdom, love, hospitality, conviction, and humility. These virtues seek the flourishing of others, not with an eye to contributing to some personal or institutional agenda, but for the sake of Christ and the person being welcomed and helped. Church-related academic institutions that embody and live out their Christian traditions will be especially well equipped to be mentoring communities — communities where concern for the newcomer permeates the ethos of the campus. Mentoring communities strive to live out Paul's exhortation to the Philippians to follow Christ's example: "Let each of you look not to your own interests, but to the interests of others" (Phil. 2:4).

Introduction

The authors of this book all have experience in designing and implementing mentoring programs at church-related colleges and universities. Our institutions are founded by and affiliated with a wide range of Protestant denominations and Catholic religious bodies. Our conversations with one another have taught us that church-related colleges and universities, no matter what their founding tradition, have many common challenges and strengths.

Well-designed programs should fit the particular institutions in which they are housed. They require careful thought about questions like: How will the mentoring of new faculty be shaped by the particularities of history and ethos of our college or university? How will mentoring nurture the specific gifts and goals of new faculty members? And how will mentoring support and enliven the particular educational mission of our church-related college or university?

Somehow or other the student must realize that education is a Christian vocation, one's prime calling from God for those years, that education must be an act of love, of worship, of stewardship, a wholehearted response to God.

— Arthur F. Holmes, *The Idea of a Christian College*, 49

We have designed this book to be of maximal use to those at all stages of involvement in new faculty mentoring. If your institution already has a new faculty mentoring program, reading this book will help you clarify the purpose and vision of your program and improve its effectiveness. If you have been given the assignment of designing a mentoring program, this book offers reflections on how mentoring should be shaped by your particular institution's mission, along with practical advice on designing and setting up such a program. If you are wondering whether mentoring is just a fad that your institution should forego, we offer reflections that will help you decide if mentoring is a worthwhile use of the institutional resources it would call upon.

Why We Couldn't Write "Mentoring for Dummies"

"Mentor" in most standard dictionaries is defined as "a wise and trusted counselor and teacher." If you can remember the anxiety and the questions that accompanied your first teaching position, you will know that

3

a wise and trusted counselor would be a great resource in making a good start. Maybe you succeeded without one. Maybe you stumbled into someone who took you under his or her wing and showed you the ropes. Or maybe you were fortunate enough to be a new faculty person at a college or university that had anticipated the need for wise counsel and had used institutional resources to provide them.

It is likely that you are reading this book because you are either considering starting a new-faculty mentoring program or interested in improving an already existing program. In either of those situations, some people might seek a "how to" book that will provide a step-by-step method for inaugurating or enhancing such a program — a sort of "Mentoring for Dummies" book. However, mentoring is a complex human art, not a simple skill for which there are quick and easy recipes. Good mentoring is an exercise in practical wisdom.

Practical wisdom is a virtue — a character trait that helps us live well. Both the classical and the Christian traditions have seen practical wisdom as a key virtue needed to inform and guide all the other virtues. Take communication, for example. There are certain character traits that make communication go well. Frankness, a willingness to speak the truth even when it might not be convenient, is a virtue. Yet tact, a sensitivity to the importance of timing and gentleness in speaking the truth, is also a virtue. Practical wisdom is the virtue that helps us discern when more frankness is needed and less tact, or vice versa. Biblical passages steeped in the wisdom tradition seek to tutor those who have some degree of practical wisdom and who are seeking more. The book of Proverbs issues seemingly contradictory injunctions: "Do not answer fools according to their folly, or you will be a fool yourself. Answer fools according to their folly, or they will be wise in their own eyes" (Proverbs 26:4-5). Someone looking for easy steps to handling fools would find this lack of clarity frustrating, but Proverbs assumes that those who are becoming wise will know which aphorism to heed under what circumstances. The book of Proverbs is not addressed to fools but to those who are on the way to cultivating the practical wisdom that guides action when no easy recipes are available.

Practical wisdom is gained through experience, not through being taught the right theory or the five or ten or twelve easy steps to reaching a goal. We cannot give you a blueprint for designing a mentoring program that fits your institution or for training mentors or for being a good mentor. What we can do is share our experience and help you notice things, so that your own practical wisdom can be honed in ways that are relevant for mentoring, training mentors, or designing programs.

What does practical wisdom need to notice as it reflects on mentoring new faculty in church-related colleges? First, that the Christian faith makes a difference to mentoring. In Chapter One we discuss both how mentoring can contribute to institutional goals of sustaining mission and explore how a Christian view of personhood should motivate, shape, and deepen mentoring at institutions that value their Christian identity.

Second, practical wisdom will notice that there are multiple Christian traditions — what Richard J. Foster calls many streams of living water flowing from a common source in Christ (Foster, 6-22). Believers in all these Christian traditions hold many elements in common — most centrally their common debt of gratitude and faithfulness to Jesus Christ — but these traditions also have distinctive histories that result in differences in theology, liturgy, polity, and ethos. There is great variety even within traditions — your college may have been founded not just by Roman Catholics but by Sisters of the Presentation of Mary or not just by Methodists but by Free Methodists. And, again, there is even variety within particular sub-traditions: the Presbyterian Church (USA) may be one denomination, but its regional synods have distinctive personalities and differing priorities, as do the scores of colleges and universities founded by or affiliated with it. Chapter Two, "All Mentoring Is Local," provides some examples about how the local culture and the specific founding tradition of a college or university can profitably inform mentoring. Because all mentoring is local,

[I]t is evident that besides the teaching, research and services common to all universities, a Catholic university, by institutional commitment, brings to its task the inspiration and light of the Christian message. . . . Catholic ideals, attitudes and principles penetrate and inform university activities in accordance with the proper nature and autonomy of these activities. . . . [I]t must be both a community of scholars representing various branches of human knowledge, and an academic institution in which Catholicism is vitally present and operative.

— Pope John Paul II,
Ex Corde Ecclesiae

5

we cannot provide recipes, but we can coach your practical wisdom to ask the right questions and notice relevant aspects of your local conditions.

Third, practical wisdom needs to discern that all mentoring is personal. Whether your mentoring program addresses cohorts of new faculty with group programs or pairs new faculty with veteran faculty in one-on-one relationships, mentoring will be a personal relationship between mentors and new faculty. Mentoring faithful to the Christian tradition will acknowledge the sacredness and uniqueness of the personhood of those being mentored as well as the humanity mentors bring to mentoring.

Mentors need practical wisdom as they exist in a complex web of relationships. They have been asked by their college to contribute in a formal way to the nurture of the college's future as embodied in new faculty. Part of their role will be to pass on the college's mission and tradition; they will also communicate its institutional priorities. But they also must negotiate the complexities of performing an institutional role while remembering that each new faculty member's good must also be a priority. The mentor is a flawed and finite person in a flawed, finite structure, trying to contribute both to institutional objectives and the personal flourishing of the new faculty person being mentored. Chapter Three seeks to hone the practical wisdom needed to meet that challenge.

Chapters Four and Five are the closest we come in this book to step-by-step procedures and "how to's," while Chapter Six is an overview of outcomes that will result from mentoring. Chapter Four addresses design issues and focuses on the decisions and actions needed to begin a mentoring program. Chapter Five addresses issues to be faced once the program is up and running. Although these chapters contain lots of specific pointers on the nuts and bolts of mentoring programs, you will still need to rely on your own practical wisdom. Because all mentoring is local, we cannot tell you how much money your university should expend on mentoring or whether your college should implement a cohort mentoring, one-on-one mentoring, or

First, all Christian nurture and education are for the sake of mission. That's why we do it. That's its purpose. Second, nurture and education are themselves forms of mission.

— Craig Dykstra, *Growing in the Life of Faith*, 159

6

mixed program, nor can we tell you whether to focus more on helping new faculty integrate faith and learning or on the spirituality of teaching. What we can do is help you think intelligently about such decisions.

How to Use This Book

We have arranged our material so that it can be of maximum help to you, striking a balance between theologically informed reflection and practical considerations. The chapters do build on one another to a certain extent, but they can also be read selectively. If your most pressing questions have to do with whether a mentoring program will be of genuine benefit to your faculty, you may want to start by reading the second section of Chapter One ("Resisting 'Missional Amnesia'") and the book's conclusion, Chapter Six, which highlight the difference that mentoring can make. These are also helpful sections for administrators concerned about funding. Such people will have legitimate questions about what the expected benefits to the institution will be if scarce resources are assigned to a mentoring program. Once they understand that a well-designed mentoring program can build collegiality and loyalty to the mission, and improve faculty retention and productivity, they will understand that funding such a program is a wise investment in the quality of the institution.

If you and your institution are already convinced that a mentoring program is worth pursuing and want to think more clearly about how to design a program that fits your particular college or university, Chapters Two and Four may be of most immediate interest to you. These chapters focus on how to think about your institutional mission and how that mission might shape the goals, priorities, and design of your mentoring program. Chapters One and Three are also foundational to thinking about mentoring in the context of Christian mission. Chapter One focuses on how a Christian context informs the conception of mentoring. We discuss how the history of church-related higher education highlights the importance of mentoring for countering what we call "missional amnesia" and how a Christian view of personhood and community should inform mentoring. Chapter Three develops the emphasis on mentoring as contributing to the discernment of individual calling. We believe that being a teacher/scholar is not just a job but can be fruitfully seen as a vocation or calling in the theological sense. Mentoring can help instill this vision in new faculty.

If you are reading this book because you are looking for ideas that could help improve an existing mentoring program, Chapter Five will be of direct help in problem solving. It addresses such practical issues as dealing with a mentoring relationship that is not working out, measuring effectiveness and making improvements, and sustaining energy and refreshing vision. Although Chapter Five offers the most direct help in addressing specific problems, reading the book as a whole will help you think in fresh ways about your institution and your program. Stepping back and looking at the big picture is perhaps the most effective way to improve your program and renew enthusiasm for the important task of mentoring new faculty. Appendix One provides questions for mentoring directors to ponder as they design, implement, and attempt to improve mentoring programs.

Mentoring for Mission also will be useful to individual mentors as programs begin and mature. The first three chapters will help mentors reflect on how mentoring at their institution might be shaped by the Christian tradition in general, by their particular institution's vision and ethos, and by the personal needs of individual faculty. Appendix Two contains questions that can form the basis of discussion during mentoring orientation and training, and Appendix Three contains questions that mentors may want to discuss directly with the new faculty whom they are mentoring.

We trust that you will learn as much from reading *Mentoring for Mission* as we have learned from facilitating mentoring programs on our own campuses and from our conversations with one another. We are deeply grateful to the Lilly Endowment for the Arts and Humanities and to the Lilly Fellows Program at Valparaiso University for the funds that have made this project possible. Their vision of practical help in nurturing the future of church-related higher education has informed and enriched our work.

BIBLIOGRAPHY

Cunningham, Shelly. "The Nature of Workplace Mentoring Relationships among Faculty Members in Christian Higher Education." *Journal of Higher Education,* 70, no. 4 (1999): 441-64.

Dykstra, Craig. *Growing in the Life of Faith: Education and Christian Practices.* Louisville, KY: Geneva Press, 1999.

Foster, Richard J. *Streams of Living Water: Celebrating the Great Traditions of Christian Faith.* New York: Harper Collins, 1998.

Holmes, Arthur F. *The Idea of a Christian College.* Grand Rapids: Eerdmans, 1975, 1987.

John Paul II. *Ex Corde Ecclesiae.* The official document, *Constitutio Apostolica de Universitatibus Catholicis,* was published by *Libreria Editrice Vaticana* in 1990. An English version was published by *Libreria Editrice Vaticana* and distributed by the Sacred Congregation for Catholic Education. It also appears in *Origins* 20, no. 17 (October 4, 1990): 265-76.

Knoerle, Jeanne, S.P., "The Love of Learning and the Desire for God," *The Cresset,* June/July 1997, 15-21.

CHAPTER ONE

Mentoring and Christian Mission

- *Remember What It Was Like?*
- *Resisting "Missional Amnesia"*
- *Mentoring: An Occasion for Grace*
- *How Does Your Garden Grow?*

Remember What It Was Like?

The U-Haul truck that she followed contained her husband and everything they owned as well as their two sons, ages six and three. They were on their way to a place that her husband had never been and that she had seen only once, during an ugly late-January thaw. The most vivid memory she had of the place was seeing ice-fishing shacks bobbing up and down in a lake of breaking ice. On this day in July, as they made their way from the west coast to the Midwestern town where she would be teaching, the woman and her husband took turns riding with their two boys for sanity's sake. The boys were with him during this stretch, and she was listening to a book on tape.

The story she heard was Isak Dinesen's *Babette's Feast*. One of its major themes is the consequence of choice and commitment — of roads taken and not taken. One of the characters in the story stands up at the feast to make a speech.

Man my friends . . . is frail and foolish. We have all of us been told that grace is to be found in the universe. But in our human foolishness and short-sightedness we imagine divine grace to be finite. For this reason we tremble. . . . We tremble before making our choice in life and after having made it again tremble in fear of having chosen wrong. But the moment comes when our eyes are opened, and we see and realize that grace is infinite. (40)

She blinked back tears of relief. These were the very words she needed to hear, given the load of mixed emotions she carried as she made her way to her new town and college and life. She was grateful to have been offered a tenure-track job at what looked like a good college and was excited at a new adventure. But she also had some major apprehensions: Would her husband, who — bless him — was moving for her sake, be able to find a position he wanted in the area? If he didn't find something that was a good fit, would she be happy enough at this college to make his sacrifice something more than pointless? Would the town be a good place to raise her children? Would faculty duties at a liberal arts college allow enough family time to sustain a marriage and help her children thrive? Could she stand living without mountains? Could she survive winters with ninety-six inches of snow? Maybe she was making a terrible mistake.

She also had apprehensions about this college's religious connections. The hiring process at the college had addressed these issues to a certain extent, and she had also done some homework — she had, for example, looked up the denomination with which the college was affiliated in the *Handbook of American Denominations*. She wanted to understand the religious identity of the college before she agreed to teach there, because she knew enough about the landscape of higher education to know that there were plenty of Christian colleges out there that would not want her and where she would not want to teach. She considered herself an orthodox Christian and was in quite a few ways theologically conservative. But she knew that orthodoxy is in the eye of the beholder and that by some people's lights she would not qualify. She did not want to feel as if she would be under continuing scrutiny to see how she measured up against an unfolding list of more and more specific and idiosyncratic doctrines. On the other hand, she knew that she would be uncomfortable teaching at a place that mouthed Christian platitudes when it served its fundraising or recruiting purposes but had no serious interest in Christianity as more than useful window dressing.

Though the college had sent her materials about its church connection and the chair of the department and others had talked to her about it during the interviewing and recruiting stages, she felt a long way from knowing what she was getting into. She had read the college's documents, but she knew that texts (especially when crafted within an academic community) have unwritten subtexts. What did the theological language in the college's mission statement mean? Did it mean reading Genesis as a history and science textbook? Did it mean seeing process theology as heresy? Did it mean just appearing Christian enough to keep the donor-base happy? "Moral turpitude" was listed as a possible condition of dismissal at the college. What *is* that here, she wondered. At some Christian colleges, moral turpitude might include drinking alcohol, dancing, or divorcing; at others it might include nothing short of being convicted of a major felony. Other questions she had concerned the relationship of her discipline to the Christian affiliation of the college. She knew that some of the questions raised by her discipline might strike some Christians as dangerous. Could she be true to her discipline without getting bad student ratings or being viewed as subversive by the administration?

So she trembled and thanked God and Isak Dinesen for reminding her that grace was infinite. As she drove she wondered where she would find a safe place to ask her questions. Would she just have to throw herself on God's grace and hope for the best?

Resisting "Missional Amnesia"

One important motive for mentoring is compassion rooted in remembering the apprehensions and confusions you yourself may have had in taking on your first full-time teaching job. Empathy can move veteran faculty to make time in their busy schedules to help junior faculty find their way in a new environment.

Remembering has also become an important institutional issue for church-related colleges and universities because of a growing awareness that it is all too easy for the Christian mission of the founders to become a fact about the school's past with little or no influence on its present self-conception or daily life. Many church-related schools have not dealt wisely with the growing number of faculty and administrators who arrive with differing degrees of understanding and appreciation of the values that undergird the founding mission of the institution. A decline of original religious impetus can come about unintentionally; in such situations, schools face the loss of their founding *raison d'être*. Within the church-affiliated university or college community, the realization has dawned that the continuation of a robust Christian context cannot be taken for granted.

"Ownership" of the mission has only recently become an issue for discussion in many religiously affiliated schools. Historically, this was not seen as necessary. If a clearly identified religious group established a school, and its members composed all the faculty and administrators, why would they wonder about who was fully invested in the mission? In Protestant schools, ordained members of the denomination formed not just the Religion or Bible department, but were scattered throughout the faculty and made up the majority of the administration and Board of Trustees. Faculty members often were required to affirm a doctrinal statement considered central to the identity of the founding denomination. In Catholic schools the religious congregation of nuns, priests, or brothers was a visible sign of the mission; the *charism* or unique character of the founding community of men or women largely determined the goals and mission of the school. The few lay faculty and administrators who were employed at the college or university were frequently attracted to the values and mission of the founding congregation and usually shared the same church affiliation. At both Protestant and Catholic institutions, chapel services and spiritual devotions were mandatory, and the educational goals of the school were intimately connected to these reminders of faith.

Changes occurring in the last century have substantially altered this picture for many colleges and universities. When the predominant influence at an institution is uniformly denominational, mission values are embedded in the life of the institution. The rituals and beliefs of the denomination are shared, expected, widely practiced, and clearly acknowledged. As these uniform practices change and the influence of secular values grows, universities and colleges are confronted with the need to reflect upon their mission or risk losing it. Faculty and administrators who once took the continuance of their religious culture and values as a certainty now are asking who is responsible for the mission, and whether the mission can thrive without more intentional efforts.

Recently, many authors who have reflected on the history and nature of American higher education have noted the forces that push church-related institutions toward secularization and loss of distinctive identity (Burtchaell; Dockery and Gushee; Hughes and Adrian; Marsden, *Soul;* Roberts and Turner; Sloan). These forces take many different forms. Reaction to perceived threats to academic freedom from those entrusted with denominational oversight, the importation of a "scientific" model of evidence for knowledge in the social sciences and the humanities, and the growing compartmentalization of the academic disciplines have affected both Protestant and Catholic schools (Roberts and Turner, 14 and *passim*).

Academic culture at large, especially the culture of most of the research universities that train Ph.D.s, does not offer help to colleges and universities that are serious about resisting missional amnesia. General academic culture often operates on the assumption that religious faith is intellectually suspect and that religious attitudes and assumptions have no legitimate place in scholarship. People of faith who pursue Ph.D.s are provided with numerous subtle and not so subtle incentives to pursue scholarship and teaching in ways that are indistinguishable from their secular counterparts (Sloan, 204, 232). The assumption that most academic subjects are and should remain religiously neutral can make faculty at church-related colleges and universities who are involved in searching for new faculty members feel awkward, and even reticent, in inquiring into the religious commitment of candidates. Even when people of faith are identified and recruited as new faculty members, these people may be inexperienced and uncomfortable with exploring the relevance of their faith to their scholarship

> *Countless colleges and universities in the history of the United States were founded under some sort of Christian patronage, but many which still survive do not claim any relationship with a church or denomination. Even on most of the campuses which are still listed by churches as their affiliates, there is usually some concern expressed today about how authentic or how enduring that tie really is; and often wistful concern is all that remains.*
>
> — James Tunstead Burtchaell, *The Dying of the Light,* ix

and teaching. Though they may be people of faith, they may also be unfamiliar with the particular branch of the Christian tradition with which their college or university is affiliated.

Because many forces in higher education pull faith and academic excellence apart, it is crucial for church-related colleges to become mentoring communities that pass on a distinctive vision of how and why the founding religious tradition of the college or university should be viewed as an educational asset. William Willimon and Thomas Naylor have argued in their book, *The Abandoned Generation,* that universities need to change in order to be more effective in helping students become genuinely educated adults. They see the large, impersonal, research-oriented university as ill equipped to help students understand the relationship between education and character or to provide the sense of community and purpose that students need to flourish. "What is missing in most colleges and universities," according to Willimon and Naylor, "is a well-defined sense of direction for administrators and faculty alike that goes beyond vague platitudes about teaching, research, and good citizenship. Why does the institution exist in the first place? Who are its constituents? What is it trying to accomplish?" (Willimon and Naylor, 58).

Many of Willimon and Naylor's recommendations for change are in fact descriptions of features that are already true of many church-related colleges and universities. They recommend a relatively small size (around 2000 students), small dorms (300 or fewer residents), institutional emphasis on teaching and on personal relationships among faculty and students, a well-defined core curriculum, and a clearly stated mission that guides administrative decisions and shapes faculty and student culture. Many church-related colleges and universities do not need to change in order to fit this description. What they may need to do, though, is be vigilant about passing on the rationale for these features to coming generations of administrators, faculty, staff, and students. If in fact the rationale for these features is informed by the religious context of the college or university, this link between religious identity and excellence in education must be illuminated for each succeeding generation of faculty and students.

Each church-related institution's particularities entail very specific priorities; each has its distinctive history, ethos, and mission. No newly recruited faculty member is likely to arrive with a full-orbed grasp of these particularities. It should not be assumed that faculty will just tumble to the significance of their college's distinctives without help. In the absence of intentional conversations about mission, an uninformed faculty culture may come to view the college's Christian tradition as a liability to be overcome or as irrelevant. Or they may not give the founding tradition much thought at all. Mentoring new faculty is one vital component in nurturing the connection between institutional mission and the everyday life of colleges and universities. It forms the foundational activity of a mentoring community that seeks to meet the needs of faculty as they begin and as they continue in their careers.

Mentoring: An Occasion for Grace

Both "mission" and "mentoring" have become hot topics in the business world, but mentoring for mission informed by the Christian tradition will be profoundly different than mentoring for mission in some businesses.

Take, for example, a fast-food franchise that posts its mission statement on a prominent wall in each of its restaurants and mentors its employees. Mentoring in such a context serves as a means to an end of delivering quality service and uniform product with the ultimate goal of maximizing market share and profitability. Veteran employees and shift managers will teach new employees how to make burgers and fries, when to discard food that has spent too much time under the heat lamp, and how to smile, make eye contact, and always ask, "Did you want that super sized?" Such businesses may seek to treat their employees fairly, but their workers are, at bottom, replaceable means to set corporate goals.

"Mentoring" of this sort would be severely impoverished both from a broadly humanistic and a Christian perspective. As valuable as resisting missional amnesia is, mentoring has to be more than a mere means to pursue this end or it will be sub-Christian. In a culture in which mentoring has been cheapened in many contexts, it is worth reminding ourselves of the original story from which we get our word "mentor."

The word "mentor" is actually a gift to us from the classical tradition, first making its appearance as the name of a character in Homer's epic poem, the *Odyssey*. The role that Mentor plays in Homer's story originally imbued the word "mentor" with its meaning. Mentor, so Homer's story goes, was an old and trusted friend of Odysseus. Too old to go off to another war when the Greeks set out to Troy to reclaim Greece's honor, Mentor is left to keep an eye on Odysseus's household. As the *Odyssey* opens, the Trojan war is long over, but Odysseus has yet to return home. Has he been lost at sea? For years, would-be suitors for Penelope (whom they would like to assume to be Odysseus's widow) have invaded Odysseus's household, abusing Greek customs of hospitality by eating and drinking at its absent owner's expense. Telemakhos, Odysseus's son, was an infant when his father left for Troy; now he is a young man, increasingly incensed at the disrespect being shown to his parents and worried over the fate of his father, but uncertain about what he can do.

Athena was nearby and came to him,

putting on Mentor's figure and his tone,

the warm voice in a lucid flight of words:

"You'll never be fainthearted or a fool,

Telemakhos, if you have your father's spirit;

he finished what he cared to say,

and what he took in hand he brought to pass . . .

. . . you will have the sap and wit

and prudence — for you get that from Odysseus —

to give you a fair chance of winning through."

— Homer, *Odyssey*, 2:282-88; 294-96

It is at this pivotal point that Mentor plays a crucial role — or a least Mentor's persona does. For in the *Odyssey,* the most crucial things done and said by Mentor are in fact done by the goddess Athena disguising herself as Mentor. As "Mentor," Athena suggests to Telemakhos that he needs to continue believing in his father's return, and must set out to search for him. As "Mentor" she then develops a plan of preparation, executing some of the plan herself and assigning other portions to Telemakhos. As "Mentor" Athena provides vision, support, resources and companionship as Telemakhos launches into his unknown future.

Mentoring is such a rich concept because the role of Mentor is to bridge. Mentor, the old and trusted friend of the father, represents tradition and memory, linking the best of the past with the unfolding future. Athena as "Mentor," the embodiment of divine insight and inspiration, represents the human capacity to incarnate, discern, and help others discern the transcendent within the mundane. Mentoring links tradition with the future through helping the coming generation become its best self. Mentor is the voice of experience, and through the voice of Mentor one sometimes hears divine insight.

Lessons learned from this pre-Christian story can inform mentoring; at the same time, these lessons can be deepened by drawing on Christian convictions. Christians share with the broadly humanist tradition a belief that human beings have dignity and infinite value; unlike secular humanists, they know that human dignity and worth are grounded in the image of God. Mentoring has a natural place at church-related colleges because a Christian institution would not, we hope, view new faculty members as "human resources," on a par with the physical plant and the institutional investment portfolio, to be shaped in the way that most benefits the college or university without regard to their own personal flourishing. Martin Buber reminds us that regarding people as mere resources is seeing them "not as bearers of a *Thou* . . . but as centers of work and effort" to be utilized for institutional purposes. (Buber, 119). To see someone as a center of work and effort, as a mere means to an end, is to see them in a sub-Christian way, even if the work and effort is supposed to have a Christian goal.

There are many biblical stories that exemplify mentoring: Jethro and Moses, Moses and Joshua, Naomi and Ruth, Paul and Timothy, and Jesus with the disciples. These biblical models informed later examples of mentoring among the desert Fathers and Mothers of the fourth century and throughout the history of the Church. Whether one remembers biblical pairs, Jesus' relationship with disciples on the road to Emmaus, or St. Teresa of Avila and St. John of the Cross, Christians are reminded that mentoring in a Christian context requires an environment that practices an ethic of care informed by virtues of love, hospitality, conviction, and humility.

> *Oh God, I thank you for the lanterns in my life*
> *who illumined the dark and uncertain paths*
> *calmed and stilled debilitating doubts and fears*
> *with encouraging words, wise lessons, gentle*
> *touches, firm nudges, and faithful actions along my*
> *journey of life and back to You.*
>
> — Marian Wright Edelman, *Lanterns*, xiii

Christian love is not mere pleasantness or sentiment; it takes the time to know and cherish others. As Dietrich Bonhoeffer reminds us, "Human love constructs its own image of the other person, of what he is and what he should become. It takes the other person into its own hands. Spiritual love recognizes the true image of the other person which he has received from Jesus Christ; the image that Jesus Christ himself embodied and would stamp upon all men" (Bonhoeffer, 36). In seeking genuine insight into the other, love patiently listens; it then encourages and seeks to be of practical help.

In contexts that call for connecting with people whom we are just getting to know or who are new to our community, Christian love is embodied in Christian hospitality. Hospitality involves sharing resources and giving practical help, but more than this it involves letting others "be" and not trying to make them into a modified version of ourselves (Palmer, *Company*, 68). It necessitates giving someone our full attention, which means more than giving up "multi-tasking" as we focus on those we welcome; it means viewing someone as a "human being rather than an embodied need or interruption" (Pohl, 178).

While Christian love and hospitality lead in the same direction, Christian conviction and humility can operate as a mutually correcting pair, helping us strike the balance that practical wisdom seeks. The virtue of conviction is so closely tied with mission for church-related colleges that it deserves an extended discussion.

People of conviction possess a considerable clarity about what matters to them. They have a sense that among their beliefs and values some are peripheral and some form the axis of their being. They know what would constitute intellectual, moral, or spiritual compromise — what would undermine their integrity. In our culture, where tolerance has become such an important value, conviction protects us from seeking peace by hiding what we believe or moving to a least common denominator in order to preserve the semblance of accord. Tolerance is itself a virtue, but each virtue needs to be guided by practical wisdom. Misguided tolerance can lead to intellectual and moral confusion, banal mass culture, and insipid discourse by encouraging murky thinking and inhibiting the expression of honest disagreement. Conviction can preserve clarity in our own beliefs and give us the courage to voice them, as tolerance leads us to allow others to express differing convictions.

Within church-related colleges and universities, it may be natural to identify conviction with religious beliefs and practices, but convictions may be of many different sorts. For example, almost everyone in the modern West holds the conviction that the scientific method is a powerful and effective way of coming to understand nature. Think of how many beliefs that we hold hinge on our belief in science. Poets must have conviction about expressive power; historians must have conviction about the credibility of documentary evidence. Lack of conviction would be an extreme handicap not just to a Christian mission but to the mission of any liberal arts college or university. How will we teach if we are bereft of conviction?

Liberal arts colleges, especially those in the Christian tradition, must be what Craig Dykstra calls communities of conviction. As Dykstra characterizes communities of conviction, they are groups of people who are connected across time and space by a body of convictions and practices that they hold in common. Such communities live out an historical drama. Dykstra points out that

> As one becomes a member of such a community, that drama is adopted as one's own. The story of the founding of the community becomes a part of one's own story. Great events that most clearly illuminate the character of the community become events in one's own history. Further, the drama does not belong solely to the past. Current members of the community recognize that they have parts to play in the continuing drama and so form their own lives as to continue its development. (Dykstra, 133)

Christians are called to be people of conviction within communities of conviction. In Deuteronomy 6:1-9, Moses instructs Israel to pass on its knowledge of God and its calling by vigilantly teaching their children. They are to talk with their children at home and abroad, in all their endeavors. As mentoring at church-related colleges seeks to nurture each new generation of faculty members, communities of conviction will be built by the sharing of personal stories, observations, and experiences.

Though communities of conviction are shaped by the central convictions and values that undergird their life together, they should not be lacking in humility. Humility reminds us that now we know only in part (1 Corinthians 13:12). Inducting new members into the community involves humility and a willingness to listen and learn from them, even if they are newcomers and bring differing perspectives. Communities of conviction, especially if they are colleges or universities, have the self-confidence to "argue about how the convictions should be formulated and expressed" (Dykstra, 133) even as they embody those convictions in the language, practices, key symbols, and metaphors that give a community's life its distinctiveness.

Humility keeps the passing on of the college or university's story from turning into indoctrination. Mentoring in a Christian context thus becomes an invitation to participate in the ongoing dialogue about the mission within the community as it seeks God's preferred future while preserving commitment to the best of its past. Mentors and mentoring programs can be a positive force in keeping dialogue over the convictions of the community constructive, so that diversity of opinion does not lead to dissention or disaffection. Humility can also make individual mentors receptive to learning from new faculty.

The importance of Christian virtues in mentoring does not entail that only Christians should be mentors. The Christian tradition recognizes common grace — God's gracious distribution of care and excellence outside the limits of the Christian community. The Judeo-Christian tradition's acknowledgment that "outsiders" can be pivotal to God's work in the world is perhaps most vividly embodied in the book of Ruth in the Old Testament. Ruth, one of only two books in the Bible named for a woman, recounts the story of a Moabite, a non-Jew. Ruth is not one of the "chosen people." Yet Ruth not only becomes an exemplar of Christian virtue; she is a link in the bloodline of Jesus.

As we will discuss in considerable detail in Chapter Two, types of church-related colleges vary in the amount of religious common ground considered necessary for being a full contributor to the college's mission. Having a hiring policy that allows for non-Christians among the faculty does not preclude being a community of conviction. We know of a case, for example, where a Buddhist faculty member at a Lutheran college is among the faculty who are most active in nurturing the school's Lutheran identity; while she herself has no desire to become a Lutheran, she has adopted her school's drama as her own. Schools that have non-Christians among their faculty should not hesitate to recruit them to be mentors as long as they are fully committed to the mission of the institution and have the requisite qualities of character. We will have more to say in Chapter Two about how what constitutes commitment to the mission varies depending on the type of school.

If mentoring is an exercise of love, hospitality, conviction, and humility, it will be an occasion for grace. Like other liberal arts institutions, those that are church-related will want to help new faculty become good teachers who view teaching as aiding the maturation of their students as whole people. Because of their Christian heritage, church-related colleges and universities acknowledge additionally that maturation has a spiritual dimension. Christian traditions recognize that teaching that addresses the whole person knows its need of grace and seeks to be an instrument of grace. This is no less true of mentoring new faculty. One goal of mentoring new faculty will be helping them see themselves as potential instruments of grace to their students; one effective means of doing this is having the mentoring relationship itself be a source of grace for the new faculty member. Catholic educational traditions may talk of this in terms of *cura personalis* or *pietas* (care for the whole person or development of character through the study of classical literature in preparation for service); Protestant traditions may talk of it in terms of discernment and growth in one's calling. Both branches of the Christian tradition point to a concept of mentoring that moves beyond instrumentalism. Mentoring in Christian contexts will strive to embody the kind of Christian love that seeks to be Christ to the other and to see Christ in the other.

How Does Your Garden Grow?

When the Christian tradition seeks to educate us in wisdom and virtue, it often relies on either story or metaphor. In striving to think in a fully Christian way about mentoring, it is helpful to call on two theologically informed organic metaphors, one from the Apostle Paul and one from St. Theresa of Lisieux. Though colleges are not churches, the Pauline passages about the nature of the universal Church as the Body of Christ can inform our view of college faculties. Paul tells us in Romans that "as in one body we have many members, and not all members have the same function, so we, who are many, are one body" (Rom. 12:4-5). Paul uses this metaphor in both Romans and 1 Corinthians to help tutor Christians in love and humility. In his first letter to the Corinthians,

If the ear would say,

"Because I am not an eye, I do

not belong to the body," that would

not make it any less a part of the body.

If the whole body were an eye, where

would the hearing be?

— 1 Corinthians 12:16-17a (NRSV)

Paul emphasizes that those who have a particular function within the Body must not look down on others who have a different function. Just as not all members of the Body of Christ make the same contribution to Christ's ongoing presence in the world, not all faculty members should be contributing in identical ways to the Christian mission of the college.

In another organic metaphor for reflecting on variety among persons, St. Theresa of Lisieux compares humanity to a garden. She says,

> I saw that all the flowers [God] has created are lovely. The splendor of the rose and the whiteness of the lily do not rob the little violet of its scent nor the daisy of its simple charm. I realized that if every tiny flower wanted to be a rose, spring would lose its loveliness and there would be no wild flowers to make the meadows gay.
>
> It is the same in the world of souls — which is the garden of Jesus. He has created the great saints who are like the lilies and the roses, but He has also created much lesser saints and they must be content to be the daisies or the violets which rejoice His eyes whenever He glances down. Perfection consists in doing His will, in being that which He wants us to be. (20)

This nineteenth-century Roman Catholic saint is often called "St. Theresa of the Little Flower" because she saw herself as more like a violet than like a rose. If we look at mentoring for mission as gardening, we will ask such questions as: How can we create the conditions that are optimal for growth of the differently gifted and varied individuals that make up our faculties? How can we cultivate a faculty culture in which all sorts of different ways of participating in the mission of the college are valued?

The gardening metaphor helps in countering the temptations within our instrumentalist culture to treat people as mere centers of work and effort and also can help counter a particular feature of many faculty cultures. Jane Smiley's comic novel about university life, *Moo*, contains a chapter called "The Common Wisdom." This chapter sketches what different groups at Moo University "know." Among the things that are "well known" among the faculty at Moo are that "it was only a matter of time before all classes would be taught as lectures, all exams given as computer-graded multiple choice, all subscriptions to professional journals at the library stopped, and all research time given up to committee work and administrative red tape." At Moo, "It was [also] well known to all members of the campus population that other, unnamed groups reaped unimagined monetary advantages in comparison to the monetary disadvantages of one's own group, and that if funds were distributed fairly, according to real merit, for once, some people would have another think coming" (Smiley, 20-21).

Smiley's irony highlights that much of a campus's "common wisdom" can be misinformation. Those who are carrying out mentoring programs need to keep in mind that there can sometimes be unhelpful parts of the "common wisdom" of church-related colleges and universities. Part of the "common wisdom" among many faculty members at some church-related institutions is that only members of some group of which they are not a part are viewed by the administration as making the preferred kind of contributions to the Christian mission of the college. To talk in St. Theresa's language, faculty members may say to themselves, "Those whom the administration prefers are the roses, but I am not a rose and never will be." Or to use Paul's language, "The so-called 'full contributors' to the Christian mission at this institution are eyes, but I am not an eye."

It is important to counter these divisive assumptions. Thinking in terms of the gardening metaphor points us to images one might see in a gardening book as a guide to planting a perennial border — a picture with many zones but no center. This image can help us emphasize the many, many ways of being part of a whole that is more valuable than the mere sum of its parts. Mentoring as gardening involves convincing faculty that the institution values a variety of ways of contributing to its mission. It also involves presenting the institution's history and mission in a truthful yet winsome way, and helping faculty members explore how their particular gifts and histories equip them for a unique and valuable contribution to that mission.

In Chapter Two we will discuss the categories of institutions that Robert Benne lays out in his recent book, *Quality with Soul: How Six Premier Colleges and Universities Keep Faith with Their Religious Tradi-*

tions. In *Quality with Soul,* Benne discusses different types of church-related institutions, some of which have very specific theological stipulations for members of their faculties. It might be natural to think that the gardening metaphor for faculty mentoring would apply to what Benne calls intentionally pluralistic institutions and critical mass institutions — schools where not all the faculty are required to hold the same basic theological views. This impression is misleading. Schools that have faith statements to which faculty must subscribe, or denominational requirements for faculty, will have relative homogeneity along certain kinds of parameters compared to critical mass and pluralistic schools. However, no matter what the hiring policy is at a school, the "common wisdom" about its administration's view may still be that some subgroup of the faculty constitutes the more valued inner circle of contributors to the mission of the college. There will be and should be variety within an institution that has required faith statements and behavior codes, though it will be of a different degree and within different parameters than the variety within critical mass and pluralist schools. There is nothing inherently wrong with a rose garden or a tulip garden, though there would be something odd and lacking about such a garden if it had *no* variety within it — no range of early, middle, and late bloomers, no range of colors, no mix of hybrids.

The philosophy underlying mentoring and faculty development should be that variety within whatever the institutional boundaries are is a highly valued institutional good. The gardening metaphor emphasizes that the goal of mentoring for mission is not to increase the homogeneity of the faculty. Rather, the goal is to help each faculty person optimally contribute in his or her own unique way to the mission of the college or university. New faculty should perceive correctly that mentoring at their institution is aimed at helping them be their best selves as they "bloom where they are planted." When this is the nature of mentoring, new faculty will be enthusiastically receptive to the gracious hospitality of the mentoring community.

BIBLIOGRAPHY

Bonhoeffer, Dietrich. *Life Together.* Trans. John W. Doberstein. New York: Harper and Brothers, 1954.

Buber, Martin. *To Hallow This Life.* New York: Harper, 1958.

Burtchaell, James Tunstead. *The Dying of the Light: The Disengagement of Colleges and Universities from Their Christian Churches.* Grand Rapids: Eerdmans, 1998.

Dinesen, Isak. *Babette's Feast and Other Anecdotes of Destiny.* New York: Vintage Books, 1988 (original copyright, 1953).

Dockery, David S., and David P. Gushee, eds. *The Future of Christian Higher Education.* Nashville: Broadman & Holman, 1999.

Dykstra, Craig. *Growing in the Life of Faith: Education and Christian Practices.* Louisville: Geneva Press, 1999.

Edelman, Marian Wright. *Lanterns: A Memoir of Mentors.* Boston: Beacon Press, 1999.

Homer. *The Odyssey.* Trans. Robert Fitzgerald. New York: Vintage Books, 1990.

Hughes, Richard T., and William B. Adrian, eds. *Models for Christian Higher Education.* Grand Rapids: Eerdmans, 1997.

Marsden, George. *The Soul of the American University: From Protestant Establishment to Established Nonbelief.* New York: Oxford University Press, 1994.

Palmer, Parker J. *The Company of Strangers: Christians and the Renewal of American Public Life.* New York: Crossroad, 1981.

Pohl, Christine D. *Making Room: Recovering Hospitality as a Christian Tradition.* Grand Rapids: Eerdmans, 1999.

Roberts, Jon H., and James Turner. *The Sacred and the Secular University.* Princeton: Princeton University Press, 2000.

Sloan, Douglas. *Faith and Knowledge: Mainline Protestantism and American Higher Education.* Louisville: Westminster/John Knox Press, 1994.

Smiley, Jane. *Moo.* New York: Ballantine, 1995.

Saint Theresa of Lisieux. *Story of a Soul.* Trans. John Beevers. New York: Doubleday, 1957.

Willimon, William H., and Thomas H. Naylor. *The Abandoned Generation: Rethinking Higher Education.* Grand Rapids: Eerdmans, 1995.

CHAPTER TWO

All Mentoring Is Local: Thinking about How Your Program Fits Your Institution

- *How Can We Tell Our Story If We Don't Know Who We Are?*
- *Who Are You? Types of Church-Related Institutions*
- *Three Examples*
  - *A Purist Denominational School: Abilene Christian University*
  - *A Catholic Critical Mass School: University of the Incarnate Word*
  - *A Protestant Denominational Critical Mass School: Concordia College*
- *Communicating Institutional Priorities*
- *Mentoring and Ownership of the Mission*

How Can We Tell Our Story If We Don't Know Who We Are?

Four tired people sat around the table. They were beginning to feel desperate. Would they ever get their work done? Their assignment was to design a mentoring program for their institution and they were up against a deadline. Having failed to find time during the regular academic year to complete their task, they were now meeting during the summer. Their president had graciously given them a stipend for this extra summer work, but now he expected results. They had realized for a long time that their greatest challenge was designing a program that would be of genuine help to new faculty in understanding the mission and ethos of their college. But what *was* the ethos and *how could* the mission be articulated in a way that would be genuinely welcoming to new faculty?

They had agreed that if they began a program that was a bad fit for their institution, it might be worse than having no program at all. That's why they weren't just importing another institution's program. A mentoring program that worked well at another institution might be quite inappropriate for them. But they needed to get clearer about who they were as an institution before the planning process could make progress. They felt stuck.

Perhaps surprisingly, their breakthrough came when one of their number, the newest faculty member present, admitted that she would not characterize herself as a Christian and wondered out loud about why she would want to teach at this particular college, let alone design its new faculty mentoring program. Maybe her presence on this committee was a mistake. Did she belong on this committee? Did she even belong at this college?

All of them quickly recognized that "Do I belong?" and "Where do I fit?" were questions that their new faculty members might have coming into the mentoring program. The discussion that ensued allowed them to articulate what they felt the ethos of their college was. They came to an agreement that the founding tradition of their college did not imply that one needed to convert faculty to that tradition in order for a faculty member to become a full-fledged member of the college. As they saw it, the founding tradition emphasized dialogue. Willingness to engage in dialogue would be the hallmark of a member of their campus community. But not just any sort of dialogue. Their college's founding tradition emphasized dialogue that would foster expansion of thought and promote continued respect for persons who had different beliefs.

They now felt they could move on to framing a telling of the institution's history and nature. That telling of the institution's mission would form the basis of one of the ongoing group activities for new faculty, in this case conducted by the campus chaplain. They knew that many church-related colleges would not see dialogue as central to their identity, at least not in the way they found it central to their own. But that was fine with them as they moved toward designing a program that fit who they were.

Who Are You?
Types of Church-Related Institutions

How would your college explain its mission and their role in it to new faculty? Would being willing to engage in dialogue strike you as a weighty enough characterization of what makes your institution distinctive?

The nature, history, and mission of your particular institution should be conveyed to new faculty through your mentoring program; they should also make a difference to its goals and design. But before you can decide what difference your mission should make for mentoring, you need a clear sense of who you are. A framework for thinking about general types of church-related institutions provides a start for such thinking. This skeletal overview will then be fleshed out by looking at three specific colleges of differing types and seeing how their distinctives make a difference in their mentoring programs. Finally, we will discuss how to balance ownership of mission with diversity of opinion within a community of conviction.

Robert Benne's book *Quality with Soul: How Six Premier Colleges and Universities Keep Faith with Their Religious Traditions* presents basic categories of church-related institutions. Benne groups institutions into four types: orthodox, critical mass, intentionally pluralist, and accidentally pluralist. *Orthodox* institutions in Benne's classification see the relevance of their Christian vision as pervasive, and they require a shared point of view among 100 percent of their faculty and staff — and many times among their students as well — on matters that they view as fundamental to their faith tradition. *Critical mass* institutions in Benne's classification give Christianity (and perhaps a specific Christian tradition) a privileged voice within the institution. They seek to have that voice embodied in a critical mass (a majority or a sizable minority) of its faculty and students. Religion courses will almost always be among the required courses at critical mass institutions, but it would not necessarily be assumed that a "Christian perspective" would be taken in all courses throughout the curriculum.

Benne sees a major divide between orthodox and critical mass institutions on the one hand and intentionally and accidentally pluralist institutions on the other. *Intentionally pluralist* schools are more likely to describe themselves as having a Christian heritage than to emphasize

Christianity or a particular faith tradition as part of their present identity. In such institutions, Christianity is one voice in the conversation, but it is not necessarily a privileged or even a very
strong voice. Hiring policy at such institutions may weigh
a candidate's identification with the institution's founding religious tradition as a factor among many others but
not as a decisive consideration. In *accidentally pluralist*
institutions there is virtually no public acknowledgement
of the institution's religious heritage. In orthodox and
critical mass institutions, a Christian vision is the organizing principle of the college or university. In pluralist institutions of both types, organizing principles have secular sources.

A tradition is a democracy in which the dead have a vote.

— G. K. Chesterton

Benne's general classifications can be elaborated by more fine-
grained distinctions. We prefer to substitute the less loaded term "purist" for Benne's "orthodox" label for institutions that seek to have 100
percent of their faculty be of a certain affiliation or belief system. It
should be noted that there are a variety of ways of being purist. Some
colleges — for example, Abilene Christian University — seek to hire 100
percent of their faculty from their founding tradition. We call these colleges and universities *Purist Denominational* institutions. Other colleges, like Wheaton College, seek to hire 100 percent of faculty members
who can ascribe to a nondenominational or interdenominational faith
statement that is evangelical in content. We call these schools *Purist
Evangelical* institutions. Finally, other colleges — Hope College, for example — might strive to hire 100 percent of faculty members who are
professing Christians but make only broad, ecumenical stipulations
about the nature of Christian faith and practice. We will call such colleges and universities *Purist Ecumenical* institutions.

In the same way that distinctions can be made among different
types of Purist schools, Critical Mass schools may be distinguished in
terms of what sort of critical mass they value. Some institutions (*Denominational Critical Mass* schools) might think it is important to have
a critical mass of people who identify with the founding denomination
of the college or university. Others (*Ecumenical Critical Mass* schools)
value preserving a commitment to the Christian faith (as variously understood and practiced in many denominations) among a sizable portion of the faculty.

Purist			Critical Mass		Pluralist
Denomina-tional	Evangelical	Ecumenical	Denomina-tional	Broadly Christian	
100% of faculty from founding denomina-tion	100% of faculty subscribe to an evangelical statement of faith	100% of faculty are committed members of some Christian church	Seeks a majority or sizable minority of members of founding denomina-tion among faculty	Seeks a majority or sizable minority of Christians among faculty	Gives affiliation with the founding tradition or Christian commit-ment little or no weight in evaluations of faculty candidates

These distinctions will cut across distinctions of the denominational identity of the college or university. Pepperdine University, for example, is a Denominational Critical Mass institution (indeed, some might see it as having many features of Intentionally Pluralist institutions). It does not require that its faculty members be members of its founding denomination (the Churches of Christ) or even identify themselves as Christian. However, members of its higher administration are members of the Churches of Christ, and the administration seeks to keep a significant number of Churches of Christ members among its faculty. Among its student body, the number of those who identify with the Churches of Christ is 15 percent — quite a bit below what many would think of as a critical mass. In fact, when students of Seaver College, Pepperdine's undergraduate school, were surveyed a few years ago, "43 percent . . . indicated that Pepperdine's identity as a Christian institution was 'of no practical consequence' for their decision to enroll at Seaver College, and 10 percent thought it was a 'minus'" (Hughes, 440). In contrast, Abilene Christian University, though also founded by the Church of Christ, is a Denominational Purist school, hiring all of its faculty members from within the Church of Christ, and recruiting most of its student body from that denomination. To take another example, Hope College and Northwestern College (Orange

City, Iowa) are both affiliated with the Reformed Church in America, yet Hope characterizes itself as ecumenical and rooted in the Reformed tradition while Northwestern calls itself evangelical and Reformed.

These examples illustrate that an understanding of "Who Are We?" will need to encompass more than just the nature of the founding denomination of the institution. It will also need to take into account the college's or university's current relationship to its founding denomination and how it conceives of itself in relation to the broader Christian community and to those outside the faith. Beyond this, it will need to take into account the makeup of the student body and the cultural setting in which the college or university is embedded. Are the students mostly eighteen- to twenty-two-year-olds, or is there a sizable portion of non-traditional students? Is the student body religiously and ethnically diverse or homogeneous? Are they professionally oriented or invested in a liberal arts conception of higher education? Is the college located in an urban environment or a small town? All these factors enter into the ethos and identity of an institution. How will that identity shape your goals and structures in your mentoring program?

Three Examples

In order to help you think about your particular institution we will present three examples of differing kinds of institutions and discuss how their institutional identities shaped their mentoring programs. The point of these examples is to stimulate you to think about your own school's nature, history, and mission, and then to ask, "What does mentoring need to be in this particular place in order to nurture our particular identity?"

A Purist Denominational School: Abilene Christian University

As has been mentioned, Abilene Christian University was founded by the Churches of Christ. The Churches of Christ, together with the Disciples of Christ and Independent Christian Churches, have their roots in the early nineteenth century Stone-Campbell restoration movement. The Stone-Campbell movement began as a Christian unity effort fol-

34

lowing the leadership of two men: Alexander Campbell, who applied Scottish rationalist philosophy to Christian thought, and Barton W. Stone, a charismatic frontier revivalist.

Stone and Campbell were two very different men, but both focused on the restoration of the simple New Testament lifestyle. Both rejected historic church traditions and hierarchy in favor of freedom for each individual to study the Bible without dependency on a professional clergy. This zeal for the "nondenominational" unity of all Christians provided a basis for the evangelistic revivals that spread throughout the pioneer country of western Kentucky, Tennessee, and the Carolinas, eventually becoming known as the Great Revival and the Stone-Campbell restoration movement. Though having their roots in revivalism, Churches of Christ have, following Campbell, "consistently prized reason over emotion and logic over speculation" (Hughes, 407). This emphasis on reason, coupled with a rigorous attachment to the biblical text, has promoted a proliferation of institutions of higher learning and produced a number of distinguished scholars.

Abilene Christian University (ACU) is the largest of all Churches of Christ universities, with a student population of over 4000. Approximately 70 percent of the students are members of the Churches of Christ. ACU is not funded by an official structure within the Churches of Christ, nor does it receive any funding from its congregations. However, ACU does depend on the good will of those congregations to promote the university to prospective students. Churches that feel the university is becoming too liberal may discourage their youth from applying. The same is true for those who see the university as too conservative.

Because all members of the faculty at ACU are members of the Churches of Christ, its mentoring efforts do not need to make orienting new faculty to the history and nature of its founding tradition a priority. It would be a mistake, however, to assume that because the full-time faculty are all members of a particular religious tradition they are equally conversant with all its relevant features. Even in a relatively homogeneous community such as ACU, collegial discussion between mentors and new faculty about the history of its religious roots is a resource and motivation for new faculty to bring faith to bear on the life of the mind.

An important aspect of mentoring at ACU is helping faculty understand some of the university's current tensions and how these are a predictable outgrowth of the history of its religious tradition. ACU, which posts its mission statement throughout its campus and has required daily chapel, sounds like a hotbed of homogeneity, yet below the surface there is considerable diversity. Founding principles, at one time thought to be inviolable, are being questioned in light of more recent scholarly inquiry. For example, the role of women in public worship creates a tension between church practices and the role of women in society today. While the university actively seeks more women to join its faculty, it grapples with new questions about the role of women in the religious life of the university. Such a situation affects the mentoring of new faculty. How will this be presented and interpreted by ACU's mentors? How will the mentoring of new women faculty help them to deal constructively with what some may see as a very difficult or confining situation and others may see as a source of comfort and peace in established ways?

Yet another aspect of ACU's identity is its location in Abilene, Texas. Texas is widely known as a place with a vivid cultural identity that differs from other parts of the United States. Faculty members from other parts of the U.S. can often feel isolated and out of place during an adjustment period. This is also true of their spouses and families. Because of this, ACU recognizes the need for what it calls "social mentoring." Social mentors are assigned to each new faculty member and are given discretionary funds to use in extending hospitality to new faculty members and their families.

ACU's mentors also help faculty balance competing institutional expectations. Faculty members' responsibility for influence on the students' faith development is recognized as equal in importance to their responsibility toward the academy and the furtherance of the professors' academic discipline. At the same time, research and scholarly expectations are a growing emphasis at ACU. Academic excellence and Christian mission are not mutually exclusive, yet they are two time-consuming priorities that create pressure on new faculty members who struggle to do justice to both. At ACU the mentor is a valuable asset in helping new faculty (1) understand concern for the student as a Christian commitment, (2) balance that commitment with the place of academic excellence as a professional commitment, and (3) learn about the historical and theological context in which those are understood in this particular place.

A Catholic Critical Mass School:
University of the Incarnate Word

We have seen how one Protestant tradition grew out of and was shaped by frontier revivalism. In contrast, much of the history of Catholic higher education in the United States is rooted in nineteenth-century European immigration. Like most Catholic colleges, University of the Incarnate Word (UIW) was born out of the poverty of the nineteenth-century immigrant church, but it has a particular drama all its own. The Sisters of Charity of the Incarnate Word first came to San Antonio, Texas, in response to a terrible yellow fever epidemic that decimated the population of San Antonio, at that time a frontier town with no hospital. San Antonio's poor were literally dying in the streets. The Bishop of Texas, Claude Dubuis, pleaded with the French order to send nuns to Texas, saying, "Our Lord, Jesus Christ, suffering in the persons of a multitude of sick and infirm of every kind, seeks relief at your hands . . ." (Slattery, 5).

In the spring of 1869, three young French women arrived with neither homes nor training as nurses nor knowledge of English or Spanish. But within six months they built a convent and a modest hospital. With a commitment to serve all people, regardless of race or creed, the Sisters admitted eight patients on the first day — four women and four men — one of whom was African-American.

Like most Catholic colleges founded by female religious orders, University of the Incarnate Word was the natural extension of work with the poor. While the Sisters' ministry started with health care, they soon realized that education was also a vital need. Bishop Dubuis, in calling the suffering poor of San Antonio "Our Lord Jesus Christ," had laid the foundation for the incarnational spirituality that infuses the University of the Incarnate Word today. Living out the belief that all life is sacred and a manifestation of God, the university remains true to the founding Sisters' values of faith in God, respect for individual dignity, and service to those most in need.

UIW's diversity in its faculty and student population is an extension of the founding Sisters' original commitment to diversity and to making education accessible. Approximately 60 percent of the student body are people of color, with the majority Hispanic. Faculty and students at UIW represent all the major world faiths. Many of the students come from poor or disadvantaged backgrounds and are first-generation college students.

Incarnate Word lets its defining characteristics, derived from the Catholic tradition together with a particular emphasis on incarnational spirituality, give direction for its mentoring program. Approximately 50 percent of UIW's faculty are Catholic, so its mentoring program, while acknowledging UIW's explicit Catholic identity, assumes that new faculty may not be sure what it means to be at a Catholic university in general and at UIW in particular.

As is appropriate at a Catholic institution, UIW has a vibrant campus ministry and meaningful liturgical celebrations. Although faculty are not expected to participate in Mass on a regular basis, there are several university-wide events that include Mass during the academic year, which faculty are encouraged to attend. Consequently, early in the mentoring program faculty discuss ways of participating in the Mass in a way that is comfortable for the non-Catholic.

Characteristics of the Catholic intellectual tradition provide the basis for lively discussion at early gatherings of new faculty and mentors. For example, because Catholic thought promotes dialogue between faith and reason, a non-Catholic sociologist may be invited to talk about the importance of religious and philosophical thinking in framing political debate about capital punishment. In this way the mentoring program demonstrates that one need not be Catholic to appreciate the long history of ethical debate and disciplined moral reasoning within the Catholic tradition. The program emphasizes the value the Catholic intellectual tradition places on intellectual diversity, affirming that contemporary societal problems are best solved by disciplined thinking based on a broad set of human and religious values. This emphasis helps new faculty see that being non-Catholic will not limit an academic career at UIW.

Permeating UIW's mission and the Catholic tradition is a concern for social justice. Students at UIW are required to participate in community service and faculty are encouraged to focus on the scholarship of social engagement. The mentoring program includes field trips to visit university-community collaboration projects and experienced faculty telling their service-learning stories, helping make the social teachings of the Church come alive for new faculty.

Because UIW's student body is more diverse than that of many campuses in the U.S., both in ethnicity and in the range of student academic abilities, UIW's mentoring program prepares new faculty for the teaching challenges presented by such diversity. The mentoring program provides sessions on the nature of UIW's student body, in which faculty share innovative teaching methods that take advantage of the various learning styles and needs of minority populations.

The particular *charism* or mission of the religious order that founds a Catholic school is embedded in the character of that institution. Franciscans, for example, emphasize the values of simplicity and helping the poor; Benedictines emphasize work, prayer, and hospitality. UIW's particular emphasis on incarnational spirituality recognizes God's presence in each person and situation. Storytelling sessions about seemingly mundane moments in the classroom in which faculty feel a glimpse of the transcendent help new faculty recognize how UIW's mission is lived daily in the classroom.

The mentoring program also models how incarnational spirituality is lived out through hospitality. Once each semester the mentoring program hosts a family potluck supper so that mentors, new faculty, spouses, and children can meet one another. Such hospitality is integral to a tradition that views the world as sacramental and each person, relationship, place, and thing as providing an opportunity for reflection of the mystery and presence of God.

A Protestant Denominational Critical Mass School: Concordia College

Like the Roman Catholic tradition, the Lutheran tradition in higher education is shaped both by its roots in Europe and its history as a product of several immigrant cultures. The Lutheran Reformation of the sixteenth century spread from Germany into Scandinavia, and the variety of Lutheran colleges is in part a function of ethnic association, with German, Norwegian, and Swedish Lutheran groups operating independently during their early histories. Two other factors in the history of the founding of Lutheran institutions are the westward movement of Lutheran immigrants and tensions over differences in emphases between pietism and a high regard for reason, both of which are legitimate aspects of the Lutheran tradition.

Concordia College in Moorhead, Minnesota, was established by Lutherans associated with the Norwegian Lutheran churches. Concordia's early agenda was to preserve the values of church and ethnic family while preparing students for effective citizenship in the new land. As time and needs changed, Concordia evolved into a four-year liberal arts college, and it has come through various mergers within American Lutheranism to be affiliated with the Evangelical Lutheran Church in America.

Concordia seeks to live out a theological understanding of education and vocation within the Lutheran tradition. For Martin Luther, education was a direct expression of justification by grace through faith. Luther saw it as necessary for the equipping of the priesthood of all believers for service in the church and the wider society. Service both to church and world required adequate education. Luther consequently advocated generalized public education for both boys and girls for the first time in Western history.

Luther's commitment to education was shaped by his doctrine of the two kingdoms. The earthly kingdom represents our place of service in the world, our vocation. The affairs of the earthly kingdom, where one is called to serve the common good, are to be ruled by reason. God's heavenly kingdom is grasped only through faith and truth as revealed in God's revelation in the biblical scriptures. Through grace, the Christian lives in both kingdoms and is called to relate to God through faith and make that faith active in love for one's neighbor. Luther did not have a dualistic conception of Christian life but rather a dialectical one. This dialectical tension allows the Christian *both* to live in the world of today and to be mindful of the world to come, to immerse herself in the life of this world through Christian freedom.

Concordia, by developing the Lutheran dialectical model of higher education in its mentoring program, helps new faculty feel liberated to explore the relationship between faith and learning without fear of encumbering either their Christian freedom or academic freedom. Faculty members who are Lutheran and those from other faith traditions are empowered to express their faith in relation to their academic work.

Concordia's yearlong mentoring program provides many opportunities for faculty to understand the Lutheran tradition in greater depth. Learning more about the history and theology of Lutheran higher education shows how it has changed since the sixteenth century. In one instance, a new faculty member from the Mennonite tradition doubted that he could appropriately talk to students about his own faith tradition because of past Lutheran attitudes toward Mennonites. It was liberating for him to learn that Lutherans no longer view Anabaptist traditions with the hostility they evidenced in the sixteenth century. Concordia's mentoring program helped him to see that the college would value his willingness to engage in faith-related questions from the vantage point of his own tradition.

Through the mentoring program, faculty from disciplines that do not seem to connect readily to faith matters, such as the physical sciences and business, come to see the implicit values present in their disciplines and the types of ethical situations in which the knowledge from their field is applied or research is undertaken. They become aware of basic assumptions that are present in all academic methodologies but which for many faculty have lain hidden or been applied unreflectively during their graduate education. Discussions of case studies in accounting, for example, open up the ethical issues in real-life situations. Physicists and life scientists bring faith to bear on discussions of the relation of creation and evolution, and in the technological application of certain scientific concepts.

The mentoring program on Concordia's campus has grown into a program that new faculty want to participate in because they have come to expect a great deal from it. It is seen as a program where intellectual growth in faith, appreciation for church-related higher education, and an increased sense of community are effected. Through it new faculty see that they can develop a sense of belonging and identity in relation to the institution.

Communicating Institutional Priorities

The ethos and distinctives of each of the three institutions whose stories we have told are embedded deeply in their founding traditions: for Abilene Christian, its blend of revivalist concern for spiritual development and rationalist concern for the life of the mind; for Incarnate Word, its social witness and sense of the sacredness of all things; for Concordia, its commitment to a dialectic that allows full participation in both

God's earthly and heavenly kingdom. These distinctives make a difference in institutional priorities. While Abilene Christian desires its faculty to make regular attendance in chapel a priority, this is not a high priority at either Concordia or Incarnate Word. Service learning, scholarship that addresses social issues, and effectiveness in teaching first-generation college students from differing ethnic backgrounds are much higher priorities at Incarnate Word than at the other two schools.

At research institutions, the three most widely used indicators for tenure decisions are numbers of publications, caliber of publications, and recommendations from outside scholars; at teaching institutions, on the other hand, the three most widely used indicators are student evaluation of courses taught, service with the university community, and number of publications.

— Carnegie Foundation for the Advancement of Teaching (quoted in Schoenfeld & Magnan, 30-31)

These differences in institutional priorities in turn shape each school's mentoring program. Yet those who designed the programs at all three schools knew that one goal of good mentoring is clear communication of expectations for new faculty. Institutional expectations must be clearly communicated in order to avoid misunderstanding, frustration, and the injustice of denying people tenure when they have in fact fulfilled the expectations that were (mis)communicated to them. Well-functioning administrative structures will see that priorities are communicated through department chairs and deans, but such structures vary in quality — sometimes even within the same institution. Mentoring programs can fill in information and reinforce messages communicated by the administration and encourage new faculty members to ask the right questions of the right people.

Mentoring programs are also a natural place to help equip new faculty to meet institutional priorities. Incarnate Word does not just communicate its desire for service learning; it exposes new faculty to a range of models for fulfilling this expectation. The mentors at Abilene Christian not only tell new faculty that they should be contributing to the spiritual growth of students; they model this concern with new faculty by being willing to engage in conversations about faith with those whom they mentor.

Mentors at all church-related colleges and universities need to understand what difference the institution expects its Christian context will make in teaching, informal faculty-student interaction, scholarship, and service, as well as what weight each of these areas is given in evaluating faculty performance. Some church-related colleges and universities pride themselves on having all faculty members integrate faith and learning in every course in every discipline. At such institutions, faculty may be expected to be able to articulate how they bring a Christian perspective to their discipline in teaching and perhaps in research and scholarship as well. Some institutions may have a question aimed at evaluating how effectively issues of faith have been integrated into courses as part of the student evaluation form. Instructors who do not send enough overt signals that they are bringing a faith perspective to their discipline may get low marks on this item of their student ratings, and this may affect their advancement at the institution. Mentoring programs at such schools will naturally focus on helping equip new faculty in these areas.

At Critical Mass schools like Concordia and Incarnate Word, explicit integration of faith into classroom settings is not a universal expectation. Yet at Concordia the mentoring program still seeks to make new faculty aware of the religious implications embedded in the practice of their disciplines. And Incarnate Word wants new faculty to take service and the quest for social justice seriously whether their motivation for it is rooted in a commitment to Christianity or has Jewish, Muslim, or humanist roots.

What are your school's distinctives and priorities? How do they or should they make a difference in your mentoring program? Do the key people implementing your mentoring program have a clear sense of what is crucial to your school's history, mission, ethos, and faculty expectations? Chapter Four and Appendix One will give you help in design or refocusing your mentoring program so that you will be able to give clear, affirmative answers to these questions.

Mentoring and Ownership of the Mission

All three of the schools we have taken as examples foster community through mentoring. They also seek to instill an understanding and ownership of their particular nature and mission among new faculty.

The mentoring program at each of these schools also has taken account of their school's particular "demographics of ownership."

Demographics of ownership include such factors as the percentage of faculty who are fully comfortable with your college's religious identity, whether faculty who personally value the mission are more likely to be senior faculty or junior faculty, and whether such faculty are more likely to be in the arts, the sciences, or the humanities. It is important to think about these matters because your school's current demographics of ownership are likely to affect new faculty at your institution. For some schools, their demographics of ownership can present challenges for mentoring for mission; for others, they may be an asset.

Consider some examples of challenges that different demographics of ownership might present. At some colleges, there are pockets of resistance (or at least indifference) to the mission of the institution. Suppose that a new faculty member is in a department that contains such a pocket of resistance. The faculty member's mentor will need to think about how to lend special help to counter the mixed messages that this faculty person may be getting from the mentoring program and the department. At other colleges, larger numbers of senior faculty may have a higher degree of ownership of the mission than newer faculty, who may have more loyalty to their professional guild than to the institutional mission. What implications might this have for the mentoring program if this is the case? Should mentors from this senior cohort be heavily utilized, or would mid-career faculty who have some degree of missional ownership be more effective role models for new faculty?

One "Ownership Map"

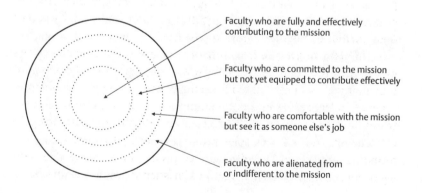

Faculty who are fully and effectively contributing to the mission

Faculty who are committed to the mission but not yet equipped to contribute effectively

Faculty who are comfortable with the mission but see it as someone else's job

Faculty who are alienated from or indifferent to the mission

In thinking through how your mentoring program can best foster broad ownership of your institution's mission, it is helpful for you to think about mapping the "ownership space" that currently characterizes your institution. In many church-related institutions, the "ownership map" would note zones that represent differing degrees of commitment to and effectiveness for contributing to the Christian or church-related mission of the college. At the center are those who are fully committed to that mission and contribute effectively to it. Further from the center are those who are committed to the mission but are not yet equipped to contribute effectively to the mission. Perhaps these people's graduate studies have given them no understanding of a Christian liberal arts context and so far not enough has been done to address this. Still further out are those who are comfortable being on the faculty of a church-related college but who assume that the Christian mission of the college is someone else's job. At the margins of the faculty are those who are alienated, and perhaps even bitter and hostile, toward the church-related or Christian aspects of the mission of the college. Perhaps this "ownership map" looks nothing like your institution. How would you redraw it to become a more accurate representation?

Although Robert Benne does not explicitly use the term "demographics of ownership," he is sensitive to how an institution's ownership map can affect efforts to preserve and especially to retrieve a robust sense of Christian mission at Critical Mass and Pluralist schools. In his final two chapters, "Keeping the Faith" and "The Long Road Back," he emphasizes that tact, discernment, and courage are needed to nurture a college's religious tradition within an atmosphere where many faculty are not communicants of the founding tradition. Institutions that aspire to use a new faculty mentoring program to enliven their sense of mission will need large doses of practical wisdom and a clear grasp of their current demographics of ownership.

In order to get a clear picture of your institution's demographics of ownership, you have to know what "ownership of the mission" means at your school. Our three exemplar schools show how different types of colleges differ in how they conceive of full ownership and contribution to the mission. At Purist Denominational or Purist Evangelical schools, "full ownership" might be viewed as adherence to the founding tradition of the college or being able to give assent to the college's doctrinal statement. At Abilene Christian it not only means being an active member of a Church of Christ; it also means being a spiritual role model for students. In contrast, at Critical Mass or Pluralist institutions, "full ownership" might be viewed as feeling comfortable within the spiritual-religious dynamic called faith or as sharing certain values that may be rooted in either a religious context or a broadly humanist one. Concordia's Lutheran heritage leads it to acknowledge that faculty may contribute fully to its mission yet have an intellectual center of gravity that is located more in the earthly kingdom than the heavenly one.

The mentoring programs at these three schools also have been sensitive to their local faculty culture. They share common goals of inviting every new faculty member to become fully committed to the college's mission and aiding every new faculty member in becoming an effective contributor to the mission. They each understand that these goals will not be facilitated by making new faculty feel somehow inadequate if they arrive without a fully articulate sense of their new home institution's mission. At Incarnate Word, helping new faculty understand ways that non-Catholics can appropriately participate in Mass is an important part of hospitality; care is taken not to send the message that it is "remediation" aimed at those who are "on the fringe." At Concordia, the mentoring program is able to present the Lutheran tradition in a way that makes a Mennonite faculty person feel more, rather than less, comfortable contributing to Concordia's mission.

What will be effective in cultivating ownership in your new faculty depends on the specifics of your faculty culture. Many schools have experimented with retreats or prayer opportunities, Bible study or theology lectures as a form of adult spiritual formation for faculty. At other schools, leading faculty in prayer may draw some uneasy feelings, and expecting them to lead prayers may send them to the library to check out the job openings advertised in the *Chronicle of Higher Education!* Such schools might be better served with a more strictly "academic" approach, informing new faculty about the religious roots of the institution and the various ways that faith can inform teaching and scholarly pursuits. Sharing the history of the founding religious body and the dedication of strong individuals who shaped the school's history may draw admiration from new faculty without making them feel pressured. A well-designed mentoring program provides a winsome invitation to participate in a variety of appropriate ways in the college's mission.

BIBLIOGRAPHY

Benne, Robert. *Quality with Soul: How Six Premier Colleges and Universities Keep Faith with Their Religious Traditions.* Grand Rapids: Eerdmans, 2001.

Hughes, Richard T. "What Can the Church of Christ Tradition Contribute to Higher Education?" In *Models of Christian Higher Education,* ed. Richard T. Hughes and William B. Adrian, 402-41. Grand Rapids: Eerdmans, 1997.

Schoenfeld, A. Clay, and Robert Magnan. *Mentor in a Manual: Climbing the Academic Ladder to Tenure.* Madison, WI: Magna Publications, 1992.

Slattery, M. P. *Promises to Keep: A History of the Sisters of Charity of the Incarnate Word, San Antonio, Texas.* Historical Studies of Hospitals, Schools in Mexico, and Incarnate Word College, vol. 2. San Antonio: Sisters of Charity of the Incarnate Word, 1995.

CHAPTER THREE

All Mentoring Is Personal: Making Sure Your Program Fits Your Faculty

- *Great Expectations; Great Frustrations*
- *Mentors Are People Too*
- *Being of Genuine Help*
- *Career Mentoring in a Christian Context*
  - *Teaching*
  - *Relating to Students outside the Classroom*
  - *Scholarship*
  - *Service*
- *Integrity: The Whole Is More Than the Sum of Its Parts*

Great Expectations; Great Frustrations

The excitement of being hired for her first teaching position! It felt wonderful. First she had learned that a prestigious academic journal had accepted a chapter from her dissertation, and now this! Between packing and moving to her new school, revising the text of her dissertation and preparing classes, she felt exhilarated and exhausted. Meeting her new colleagues and settling into a new office and apartment were a blur.

Her first classes brought her up short.

She felt as if she didn't speak the same language as her students. They were looking at her, but she didn't see anything but blank stares.

She began to panic and could feel herself racing through her planned introduction and notes. The more she talked, the more distant she felt from her students. Shaken and embarrassed, she returned to her office and prepared for her next new class later in the day. Despite her efforts, the second class was a repetition of the first disaster. When she returned to her office, she closed the door and began to cry. She should never have taken this job so far from home!

She pulled herself together when she heard someone knocking on the door. It was her mentor. He had already walked around campus with her and shared a coffee a couple of days earlier; now he was dropping by to ask her about her first classes. When she began to describe the sinking feeling she had after two horrible beginnings, he laughed knowingly. She told him she felt as though she were speaking a different language from that of her students. To her surprise, he agreed! She was speaking the language of academic and professional expertise she had learned during her doctoral studies, he told her. It was time to translate, and he would help her. He also reminded her about the special mentoring session the following week that would address "who our students are." That would help as well. Now maybe a walk was in order and another cup of coffee. He reminded her never to judge a semester by the first day. It always gets better.

Several years later, when she was asked to mentor a new faculty member in her division, she was delighted to pass on the favor she had received from her mentor. She already knew one thing she was going to build into her activities with the new teacher. She would meet before the first day of class and talk about how to begin a course. Maybe she could save someone from the sinking feeling of a bad start, maybe she couldn't. But she was willing to try.

Mentors Are People Too

The ideals concerning mentoring embodied in the classical and Christian traditions, discussed in Chapter One, may inspire us. However, for some, the very loftiness of these ideals may also intimidate. Those considering becoming mentors may think they lack sufficient humility, hospitality, conviction, wisdom, or love. The fact that mentoring is informed by the specifics of an institution's founding tradition may also make mentors feel like they have much to learn before they are worthy to "pass the torch" of the institutional vision. As Moses urged God to recruit a leader for Israel who was more eloquent than he, as Isaiah pleaded his inadequacy for his prophetic assignment, those who are asked to mentor others may say, "Find someone wiser, more sensitive, more savvy than I."

But the Christian tradition emphasizes that again and again grace comes through imperfect people. And just as giving a cup of water can be an act of grace, many of the tasks of mentoring are within the capacities of many, perhaps most, veteran faculty members. William Cutter, in his essay "A Theology of Teaching: Confluences and Creation," advocates a "theology of imperfection" that acknowledges our limitations — and the limitations of those we teach and mentor — as we seek to help one another become our best selves.

We should not forget that St. Theresa's garden metaphor, which we discussed in Chapter One, applies just as appropriately to mentors as to new faculty. Different mentors will bring differing styles and strengths to the mentoring relationship. If you have been asked to mentor a new faculty member or to serve as a resource person in mentoring a cohort of new faculty, your institution has recognized that you do have a considerable grasp of what new faculty need to know and do have the character traits of a good mentor. Yet just as we continue to gain new understanding of our discipline by teaching, so we will deepen our understanding of our home institutions and grow as people through mentoring new faculty.

Mentors who wish to think more systematically about how they conceive of mentoring within their particular institution will find helpful reflection questions for mentors in Appendix Two. The rest of this chapter will give a general overview of central issues in mentoring new faculty.

Being of Genuine Help

At the most basic level, a mentor seeks to be of genuine help to the person being mentored. This need not mean that a mentor "knows it all" or comes to the mentoring relationship with a detailed agenda. Lois Zachary emphasizes that adult learners (and new faculty members are

adult learners *par excellence*) learn best when they are involved in diag-
nosing, planning, implementing, and evaluating their own learning;
they need to be self-directed (Zachary, 4-5). She notes that mentors are
more effective if they view themselves as facilitators (a "guide at the
side") rather than authority figures (a "sage on the stage").

Who the new faculty person sees herself as (and as aspiring to become) should be a major factor in focusing the objectives at which
mentoring aims. The role of the mentor is to help the new faculty person understand the particular ecology of his institutional garden
and to discern his particular place within it. Good mentoring
will encourage a new faculty person to shape her own personal balance among scholarship, teaching, and service
within parameters that will be valued at her particular college or university. To paraphrase an often-repeated quota-
tion from Frederick Buechner, assuming that God has
called someone to be a faculty member at a particular institution, her calling is to carry out her duties in the way
that her deep gladness and the institution's deep hungers
meet (*Wishful Thinking*, 95).

Neither the hair shirt nor the soft berth will do. The place God calls you to is the place where your deep glad-ness and the world's deep hunger meet.

— Frederick Buechner, *Wishful Thinking*, 95

As new faculty seek to understand the "garden" in
which they have been planted, they must be oriented to
the institution's history and mission. For new faculty who
arrive completely unfamiliar with the founding religious
tradition of the college or university, a felt need may be for
some sort of translation manual to decode the insider language that gets thrown into college-wide discussions. Mentoring
that addresses this need can function as an entrée into deeper and
more extended conversations about the religious identity of the institution.

In this context of exploring missional commitments, a developmental model proposed by Sharon Daloz Parks can be helpful. New faculty members come in all ages and in a range of personal maturity levels. A faculty member who is new to a particular institution but who has
taught elsewhere for a number of years, especially one who worked in
other settings before pursuing graduate studies, may be in his thirties,
forties, or beyond. On the other hand, new faculty who are being hired
for their first full-time teaching job directly out of a graduate program
and who began their graduate study directly after college may be in

their twenties. Because of this, thinking about the nature of young adulthood can illuminate issues faced by new faculty.

In her recent book *Big Questions, Worthy Dreams,* Parks characterizes two developmental categories between adolescence and mature adulthood. Mature adults, she says, have convictional commitments; they believe what they believe and value what they value with considerable stability and passion because their beliefs and values arise out of a conscious process of reflection and personal commitment (70). In contrast, adolescents tend toward either a rigid dualism or an unqualified relativism. Parks, building on the work of William Perry, James Fowler, and others, elaborates on their models by observing that few people move directly from adolescence to mature adulthood. It is more common for people to pass through a stage of probing commitment (young adulthood) and tested commitment (tested adulthood) before arriving at maturity. Probing commitments are characterized by an exploratory and tentative nature that results in a series of short-term experiments in commitment. "One explores many possible forms of truth — as well as work roles, relationships, and lifestyles — and their fittingness to one's own experience of self and world" (67). At the stage of tested commitment, one's commitments have "a sense of fittingness, a recognition that one is willing to make one's peace and to affirm one's place in the scheme of things (though not uncritically). In the period of tested commitment, the self has a deepened quality of at-homeness and centeredness — in marked contrast to the ambivalence or dividedness of the earlier period" (69). Parks's focus is on applying these insights to college-level teaching, as faculty help students move toward mature adulthood. However, her observations suggest applications to new faculty members themselves.

Faculty members in their twenties and thirties may fit Parks's descriptions of tested adults or young adults, still exploring issues about who they are as workers and what matters most to them. New faculty members who are young adults or tested adults may still be exploring issues of personal commitment, religious commitment, and professional identity. If so, it will be appropriate for mentors to address issues of personal exploration with them.

Parks's characterizations of the stages of probing commitment, tested commitment, and convictional commitment may be more broadly applicable to new faculty members' commitment to their new home institution, even for mature new faculty. For experienced faculty members arriving at new institutions, mentoring may be a matter of helping them fine-tune their professional identity vis-à-vis that of their new college or university, and of helping them in the process of becoming fully at home — that is, in seeing how the institution's story can become part of their own story. This process is likely to move from an initial introduction to various tellings of the institution's story through "trying on" various ways in which the faculty member's story can fit into the larger story (probing commitment) through reflective affirmation of the institution's story (tested commitment) to being fully at home (convictional commitment). Good mentoring programs will aim at facilitating this process.

For some new faculty, the issues they consider most pressing will not be at the level of institutional commitment but will be more personal and individual. They may want to know how to avoid getting caught in the middle of an ongoing conflict among senior members of their department, how to give adequate time to their families while still meeting professional expectations, or how to weather a short-term or extended personal crisis without adverse effects on their institutional survival. In such cases, the mentor should not attempt to function as a therapist, but can provide a listening ear and, where appropriate and requested, friendly advice.

New faculty who are coming from very different parts of the country or the world may also need help in understanding and appreciating the local culture. For example, those moving from an urban setting to that of a small college town may be in for culture shock. This may be particularly true of minority faculty if their particular ethnic group is severely underrepresented in the surrounding community. Mentoring programs should be prepared to help deal with these issues.

Mentors and directors of mentoring programs should ask new faculty what areas they would find it most helpful for the mentoring relationship to address. The answers to this question will not only vary among new faculty members, but are likely to vary over time for each person as new challenges present themselves.

Whatever the focus of a particular mentoring relationship may be, respect for confidentiality will facilitate being of genuine help. A mentor who listens without feeling the need to report to a department chair or dean will help the dialogue between the new and veteran faculty member to be honest. If there is friction between colleagues, a mentor can be a safe haven in which the new colleague can tell his tales of woe. The mentor can speak openly about the "edges" at the school, those academic and political areas that call for navigational skill. The mentor may be able to explain the background of feuds or the history of jockeying for power within the institution. Having that information will help the new faculty member make wise judgments about when and if to take sides or step into the middle of an issue.

While mentoring should be tailored to needs voiced individually by new faculty members, there are two clusters of issues that can be predicted to arise for most new faculty. One of these is related to career development, which in a Christian context will include the personhood of faculty members. The second cluster of issues concerns personal integrity, remaining a whole person while performing many demanding roles.

Career Mentoring in a Christian Context

New faculty members, especially if they are coming directly from graduate school, may feel overwhelmed when they realize the full extent of their duties. A poorly designed development program for new faculty may exacerbate rather than ameliorate new faculty members' anxiety about whether they can meet institutional expectations. It is not uncommon to showcase an institution's best teachers at workshops to enhance teaching, to applaud the institution's most widely acclaimed scholars and most successful grant writers at gatherings designed to encourage research, and to spotlight the institution's most steadfast and hardworking institutional servants in celebrations of successful institutional initiatives. New faculty may observe these institutional heroes and see that they cannot excel in all of these areas at the same time and still be a spouse, a parent, a friend, a church member, and a sane and balanced human being.

Lest this be totally demoralizing, mentors should help new faculty members understand that not many in their position do all things optimally well and that making choices among priorities, which may shift over time, is appropriate. Mentors can model this for new faculty members by reflecting out loud on how they have thought through their own priorities, how they budget their own time, and what they have said "no" to in order to be able to concentrate on other things. Their goal will not be to have the new faculty members make the same choices that they have, but to help them see that choices can and should be made.

In most institutions, the choices will not be a matter of teaching *or* scholarship *or* service, but a matter of deciding how much energy one should expend in each of the three areas, and shaping one's choices within each area. Mentors can facilitate reflection on issues of balance and also provide coaching about these three traditional areas of faculty contribution. At church-related liberal arts institutions, relating to students outside the classroom is an additional important area that mentoring should address.

Teaching

Most church-related colleges and universities make effective teaching a top priority in their evaluation of new faculty members. New faculty need to become as good as they can be in the classroom in order to flourish within such institutions. Moreover, teaching will be a much more satisfying aspect of faculty life if new faculty find a teaching style that fits both themselves and their students.

As Parker Palmer has pointed out in *The Courage to Teach,* teaching can be frightening and thus requires courage. Because teaching is such a personal activity, if students seem to reject us as teachers, that can feel like a very personal rejection indeed. Students, through their reactions to us, have the power to make us feel like we are "at the top of our game" or like we are doing something that has little point. Teaching will be a frustrating experience if it is not done effectively, both for the students and the teacher.

Mentoring may include more than helping the new faculty person make wise decisions about how much emphasis, time, and energy to give to teaching. It may also focus on aiding new faculty in discerning how to find a teaching style that both fits their own interests and personality and enhances learning among the particular kind of students enrolled at their home institution. It will also contain large doses of encouragement. Jane Tompkins, in her autobiography of teaching, *A Life in School,* writes, "If nothing else, I wish I had been warned about what an ego-battering enterprise teaching can be" (90). Mentors should convey to new faculty that days when things just do not "come together" are a normal part of growing as a teacher.

Most people need and seek approval by others; faculty are no exception. But the concrete affirmations needed to sustain good teaching are unpredictable, often not there when needed, and too spare when they come.

— John B. Bennett, *Collegial Professionalism,* 59

Most faculty were in fact good students when they were undergraduates — hardworking, dutiful, and compliant, perhaps even in the face of finding more than one of their instructors boring or hard to follow. New faculty who arrive with relatively little teaching experience may be startled to find that their classes are not filled with students who remind them of themselves. Moreover, the teaching style that comes most naturally to them is likely to be copied from the teachers from whom they most enjoyed learning. Such a style may be well received and very effective with those of their students who are most like them, but it may leave other students cold. Effective mentoring of new faculty will help them find how to be their best and most effective selves in the classroom by helping them find the intersection between how they enjoy teaching and how their students enjoy learning.

Mentoring for effective teaching also addresses such basic issues as how to talk to students before class and after class, how to clarify goals for learning at the beginning of class, how to listen and reflect on class activities, and how to relax, be open to evaluation, and enjoy teaching. As Gerald Gibson notes in *Good Start,* teachers must learn how to motivate students — not just lecture — by using projects, simulations, internships, experiential learning, small groups, in-class presentations and debates, and individualized learning projects to make class stimulating and interesting.

Most faculty members grow as teachers through experimentation and experience. A "theology of imperfection" will give permission to experiment, with an assurance that failures will happen and are a natural part of growth. New faculty should be helped to acquire proficiency at a variety of teaching styles and strategies, but no faculty member can be all things to all students. Some new faculty may be good at motivating students but end up spending inordinate time on grading. Other new faculty may see themselves as very good at structuring course material and methods of student accountability but have a hard time winning the interest of students to their subject. Faculty members are likely to be most effective if they balance using a variety of teaching styles with emphasizing their own strengths. Discerning their strengths may be aided by having a mentor observe their teaching and discuss it with them afterwards. The conversation should center on what the new faculty person's goals were for the class period, what the strategies were for meeting those goals, and what they thought worked well and what they wish had gone better.

Having new faculty observe their mentors and perhaps other senior faculty in the classroom can also be useful. This is a way of generating ideas about strategies with which to experiment. It is also a way of reminding oneself what hard work it is to be in the student's shoes. Having a discussion in which the new faculty person can give feedback to his mentor may not only be helpful to the mentor but also will make the mentoring relationship a matter of peer review, reinforcing the idea that the mentor is open to learning from the new faculty person.

Relating to Students outside the Classroom

Many church-related colleges and universities pride themselves on the personal attention that their faculty and staff give to students. For faculty, such personal relationships often go beyond academic advising and interactions concerning course work during office hours. New faculty may need help in reflecting on how much time they will spend with students outside the classroom and in what ways. Mentors can help them show genuine care for students without having their personal boundaries violated.

Issues for possible discussion here are various: Will the new faculty person invite students to his or her home? How many, how often, and in what contexts? Should the new faculty member say "yes" to an invitation to become a faculty advisor to a fraternity or sorority? How much time should the new faculty member spend talking about personal troubles with a particularly needy student? Under what circumstances should new faculty members refer students to a counseling center or to campus ministries?

At many church-related institutions, mentoring will also address expectations and local customs concerning faculty involvement in the spiritual life of students and the campus community. Is frequent or regular chapel attendance expected? Is prayer viewed as a private or liturgical matter on your campus, or do faculty pray with students in their offices on appropriate occasions? Will asking individual students about issues related to their spiritual growth be viewed as appropriate interest or as an intrusion? At Purist Ecumenical, Critical Mass, and Pluralist schools, mentors will need to be available to help faculty whose religious background might make them less comfortable conforming to the campus norms discern how to comport themselves.

New faculty may be particularly concerned about how to be genuinely caring toward students without running the risk of being misinterpreted or tempted toward sexual harassment or inappropriate romantic attachment. New faculty may want to discuss with their mentors whether always to keep their office door open when a student is present, whether and when it is advisable to have a one-on-one cup of coffee with a student of the opposite sex, and how to handle situations in which a student is displaying signs of infatuation or where the faculty member feels inappropriately drawn to a student. Mentors will want to be apprised of their institution's policies and practices regarding sexual harassment, be aware of informal campus norms on such matters, and provide a listening ear if the new faculty member seeks advice.

Yet another issue that mentors may want to address with new faculty is ethical and legal guidelines for disclosure of confidential information. How, for example, should a faculty member handle a situation in which a student reveals that he is suicidal or that he has been harassed by a teacher or another student? Can and should the faculty person report this matter unilaterally? Must the student's permission to disclose be obtained? Institutions should have clear guidelines, concordant with any relevant state or federal laws about disclosure, concerning when and to whom such confidential information can be revealed permissibly.

Scholarship

Many new faculty members fear that teaching will suffer if they attempt to be "productive," and they have no idea how much and what sort of writing is satisfactory for tenure. Old slogans like "publish or perish"

*The virtues of hospital-
ity and thoughtfulness can be
ignored, even violated, in scholarship as well as teaching. Overly documented, inaccessible, impenetrable, or
opaque writing and talking obscure the
public moment that both scholarship
and teaching demand.*

— John B. Bennett, *Collegial
Professionalism,* 120

heighten anxiety without giving guidance. New faculty members are likely to need help in thinking through how to design a research agenda that is realistic within a liberal arts setting with its consequent teaching load.

As in the case of teaching, there is more than one question regarding scholarship — not just "How much is enough?" but "What kinds of scholarship does my home institution value?" and "What kinds of scholarship will I find most satisfying?" Here, as in other areas, one wants to meet institutional expectations but, more importantly, one wants to look back on one's scholarly accomplishments and see them as the product of time well spent. Mentors will want to help new faculty think intelligently about how to pursue a program of research, publication, or artistic performance that fits both the institution and the individual faculty member, acting as a professional "sponsor" or coach by advising the new colleague as she develops a research agenda and a professional portfolio.

Gerald Gibson recommends that new faculty create a plan for scholarship such as developing a product — a presentation, publication, or performance — every year or every other year. Robert Boice's research on faculty life confirms how easy it is for teaching loads to push research to a permanent back burner. Often, too little is done to help people establish early patterns of productivity and publication (81-85). Because teaching occurs daily it takes precedence over writing, which can be more easily become an object of procrastination.

Boice also found that faculty who did write were those who had balanced work habits and a positive attitude toward students, colleagues, and writing (98). Scholarship can strengthen one's teaching by keeping a faculty member current and alert to feedback, promoting discussion of scholarship and teaching with colleagues, and providing the impetus to rework courses.

New faculty members need role models who write, teach, and are collegial. They also need frequent encouragement and a clear understanding of the institutional and personal rewards of scholarly activity. It is important to develop the habit of working on scholarly activity each week during the early semesters of teaching. If this habit is not begun early in the academic career, it may be put off or even forgotten entirely. Lack of scholarly productivity can become an embarrassment for the new faculty member and may lower self-esteem and career satisfaction.

Traditionally, there has been an understood hierarchy of types of scholarly products. At the top of this hierarchy are refereed books published by leading academic presses and refereed articles in prestigious scholarly journals. Below these come book chapters, textbooks, non-refereed or semi-professional articles, and scholarly critical book reviews (Schoenfeld & Magnan, 239). In addition to these, serving on editorial boards of scholarly journals, making presentations at professional meetings, and refereeing books and articles are also considered important.

What some fail to recognize is that scholarship, when well done, is itself a form of teaching, and can teach in a variety of useful ways — not just in the scholarly monograph accessible to a few specialists in a particular field but in a variety of other publications and media. Ernest Boyer's important book *Scholarship Reconsidered* helped to bring a broader and more creative perspective to the issue of what scholarship is and what among the many things faculty members do should "count" in this category for purposes of institutional evaluation. What research universities have traditionally emphasized is the scholarship of discovery — that is, making new contributions to the fund of human knowledge. Boyer advocates recognizing other kinds of scholarship alongside this, which may be viewed as equally valuable and in some cases more appropriate to the liberal arts college. The three other categories that Boyer discusses are the scholarship of integration, which makes new connections among already extant bodies of knowledge, often across disciplinary lines; the scholarship of application, which applies extant knowledge in a creative way to new practical problems; and the scholarship of teaching, which might include producing textbooks or novel approaches to conveying knowledge to students. Boyer's conception of scholarship reveals rich connections among teaching, scholarship, and service.

Many new faculty members may feel that they need advice on how to make their research and their teaching less disjointed from one another. The conventional wisdom that all types of research enhance all types of teaching is a fine theory, but may not be borne out in practice. New faculty may need help in judging which of their research interests can be brought into the undergraduate classroom and how this can be done.

At church-related institutions, the kinds of scholarship and publication that are valued will not be utterly dissimilar to those valued in the academy in general. Most church-related colleges and universities want at least some of their faculty to be recognized for their excellence in the wider academy. The kind of publications that will be read by leading experts in one's discipline will thus be as valued by church-related institutions as by any other. Beyond these, however, a church-related college may value at least some of its faculty members being "scholars for the Church" — writing about matters of intellectual import for a wide range of educated clergy and laity. The new faculty member needs to identify and reflect on the "pecking order" of types of research produced at her home institution and decide to what extent that will shape her own research agenda. Mentors can facilitate this reflection by knowing their own institution's priorities and encouraging new faculty members to engage creatively with them.

A mentor will have the experience to know when a new faculty person is taking on too much or proposing projects too large for the university to sustain. The mentor will encourage the use of resources, grants, and any special fund for new faculty projects. The mentor can be realistic and yet encouraging. Each paper accepted, each grant gained, may be met with a cup of coffee or at least a congratulatory email.

Even though the mentor and the new faculty member may have different professional affiliations, the mentor would be wise to tutor the new colleague in the importance of one's guilds. It is important to pay one's dues, to keep memberships current, to stay in touch with what is happening in the outside world. Teaching at church-related institutions (and smaller schools in general) can be limiting in terms of contacts with the larger professional world because of limitations on time and travel money and teaching assignments that tend to make generalists out of specialists. The guild can remind a faculty member of the general trends of the discipline, the latest debates, the key works a faculty member should read.

Service

The category of service may be one of the most baffling to new faculty members. They may come from a graduate school culture that has disparaged committee work as busywork, to be avoided whenever possible and given scant attention when it cannot be completely dodged. New faculty may also be confused about what "counts" as service at their new home institution. Should anything that contributes to the growing good of the institution and the world be noted on annual self-evaluations or in tenure and promotion files?

Clay Schoenfeld and Robert Magnan have this advice to offer concerning service: "To count as 'service' for promotion to tenure, your extra-campus activities must be related directly to your academic expertise. Teaching a Sunday School class, leading a scout troop, or chairing a parents-and-teachers committee doesn't count" (51). This observation would certainly hold at a research university and would also be likely to hold at liberal arts colleges that are not church-related. It may hold at some church-related colleges and universities as well. However, some church-related liberal arts colleges may value leadership within the faculty person's own parish, congregation, or denomination, even if that service is not directly related to the faculty person's academic discipline. Here as elsewhere, mentors should be accurately informed in order to be able to give useful advice.

Connected with the issue of deciding where to serve is the mentor's role in explaining the tangled web of faculty governance. At most academic institutions, the faculty "owns the curriculum" because faculty and administrative boards and committees create policies that shape the curriculum. New faculty members need to know these policies, of course, but also how these policies are created and changed. If a new faculty member thinks that grading policies need to be addressed, where does she go? If the institution is undergoing a general education curriculum review, what part can or should a new faculty member play in the debates? If there are heated campus controversies, how does a new faculty member exercise integrity on matters of great importance without committing vocational suicide? A good mentor can help think these issues through.

The mentor, by the very fact that he or she is giving his or her time to the mentoring relationship, also functions as a role model of someone who serves. At healthy institutions of higher learning, service on campus and beyond should grow out of a sense of calling to contribute to what has abiding significance. New faculty members, in deciding what service opportunities to invest in, should ask themselves, "How can I contribute to what matters most?" not "Will I be able to list this on my vitae under 'Service'?" Mentoring, both by explicit conversation and by modeling, can help foster this attitude in new faculty members.

Integrity: The Whole Is More Than the Sum of Its Parts

For institutions that care about carrying out their life within a Christian context, faculty members will be recognized to be more than the sum of their roles. Each faculty member is more than just a teacher and a scholar and an advisor and a committee member and a charitable board advisor and a faculty liaison to a student organization. Mentoring can help new faculty members wear many hats with good grace, rather than being fragmented and pulled in all directions at once. The mentor can help the new colleague make choices to maintain a balance in all aspects of the professional life. How many hours ought one to devote to lecture preparation? How can one carve out an afternoon a week to work on an article? How many committee assignments should one accept? Is it better to stand for election to a faculty-wide committee or to serve on a specially assigned task force? In other words, where should one put one's time? Contentment as a teacher and a scholar may well depend on the ways in which one learns to deploy personal resources.

In the typical professional consciousness one's sense of underlying meaning, of essential connections with others, and of personal integration is left unsupported — leading inevitably to loss of wonder and excitement.

— John B. Bennett, *Collegial Professionalism*, 50

Faculty burnout is all too common and no less common in church-related institutions than elsewhere. A frequent cause of burnout is a sense of having lost one's self in the shuffle of the demands on one's time. The Judeo-Christian concept of Sabbath needs to be genuinely lived out. All too often, faculty — including veterans, but especially new faculty — cannot let go of their busyness and leave space in their lives for rest, re-creation, and worship. One of our home institutions held a faculty retreat where they prayed, "Teach us the art of taking minute vacations — of slowing down to look at a flower, to chat with a friend, to pat a dog, to read a few lines from a good book." Sometimes the best thing a mentor can do for a new faculty member is urge him to slow down in order to reflect on who he is.

There is an important clue as to whether one is carrying out good work. Doing good work feels good. Few things in life are as enjoyable as when we concentrate on a difficult task, using all our skills, knowing what has to be done.

— Gardner, Csikszentmihalyi, and Damon, *Good Work,* 5

Mentoring can go beyond these issues of balance and help new faculty members reflect on their individual calling as the center that holds all their various roles together and makes sense of the whole of their lives. David Gushee has rightly observed that the most important thing a professor does is incarnate a way of life ("Attract Them by Your Way of Life"). When mentors help new faculty members reflect on the question "Who are you?" they should strive to help them see that the choices they have made about how to spend their time, what to take on, and what to say "no" to, as well as the style with which they carry out their various roles, can and should come out of a centered sense of self. New faculty should, as Parker Palmer reminds us, be encouraged to "let their life speak" (Palmer, 2000) as an inner voice of wisdom to guide personal and professional choices.

BIBLIOGRAPHY

Bennett, John B. *Collegial Professionalism: The Academy, Individualism, and the Common Good.* Phoenix: Oryx Press, 1998.

Boice, Robert. *The New Faculty Member: Supporting and Fostering Professional Development.* San Francisco: Jossey-Bass, 1992.

Boyer, Ernest L. *Scholarship Reconsidered: Priorities for the Professorate.* Lawrenceville, NJ: Carnegie Foundation for the Advancement of Teaching, 1990.

Buechner, Frederick. *Wishful Thinking: A Theological ABC.* New York: Harper & Row, 1973.

Cutter, William. "A Theology of Teaching: Confluences and Creation," *The Melton Journal: Issues and Themes in Jewish Education* 27 (Autumn 1993): 18-21.

Gaede, Stan D. "The Christian University in a Divided Society." In *The Future of Christian Higher Education,* ed. David S. Dockery and David P. Gushee, 81-94. Nashville: Broadman & Holman, 1999.

Gardner, Howard, Mihaly Csikszentmihalyi, and William Damon. *Good Work: When Excellence and Ethics Meet.* New York: Basic Books, 2001.

Gibson, Gerald W. *Good Start: A Guidebook for New Faculty in Liberal Arts Colleges.* Bolton, MA: Anker Publishing Company, Inc., 1992.

Gushee, David P., "Attract Them by Your Way of Life: The Professor's Task in the Christian University." In *The Future of Christian Higher Education,* ed. David S. Dockery and David P. Gushee, 137-53. Nashville: Broadman & Holman, 1999.

Palmer, Parker. *The Courage to Teach: Exploring the Inner Landscape of a Teacher's Life.* San Francisco: Jossey-Bass, 1998.

Palmer, Parker. *Let Your Life Speak.* San Francisco: Jossey-Bass, 2000.

Parks, Sharon Daloz. *Big Questions, Worthy Dreams: Mentoring Young Adults in Their Search for Meaning, Purpose, and Faith.* San Francisco: Jossey-Bass, 2000.

Schoenfeld, A. Clay, and Robert Magnan. *Mentor in a Manual: Climbing the Academic Ladder to Tenure.* Madison, WI: Magna Publications, 1992.

Tompkins, Jane. *A Life in School: What the Teacher Learned.* Reading, MA: Addison-Wesley, 1996.

Zachary, Lois J. *The Mentor's Guide: Facilitating Effective Learning Relationships.* San Francisco: Jossey-Bass, 2000.

CHAPTER FOUR

Getting There from Here

- *Do You Just Want to Take a Stab at What Might Work?*
- *Setting Goals and Priorities*
- *The Importance of "Safe Space"*
- *Identifying Areas for Mentoring and Thinking about Program Design*
- *Group Mentoring and Individual Mentoring*
- *Considering the Pros and Cons of Mandatory Participation*
- *Addressing Budgetary and Administrative Issues*
- *Identifying and Recruiting Good Mentors*
- *Mentoring Mentors*

Do You Just Want to
Take a Stab at What Might Work?

When the dean asked her to design a more fully developed mentoring program, the first question she asked herself was, what was missing? What kind of mentoring program would aid faculty in being successful at her college? She decided to divide the program into two fairly equal sections: (I) Life within the Christian College; and (II) Life of the Mind.

"Life within the Christian College" consisted of dinner meetings with panel discussions. She invited emeritus and current faculty to reflect on the history and the nature of the college. After another dinner they talked about the Christian character of the institution. During the spring term they talked about pedagogical issues: syllabus preparation, classroom problem diagnosis, tenure and promotion, and coping with stress. There were short reading assignments, questions to prompt panelists, and a chance for new faculty to ask questions. "The Life of the Mind" consisted of luncheon discussions of two books, one for each semester. They read Wallace Stegner's novel *Crossing to Safety*, which traces the career and friendship of two couples within an academic setting, and Jill Ker Conway's autobiography of her career as an academic administrator, *True North*.

She asked new faculty to write follow up comments or questions on both components of the program. These showed that the "Life within the Christian College" component had been relatively successful, providing an environment that was relatively safe for discussion and frank questions, but that "The Life of the Mind" was much less well received. She learned that simply providing new faculty with a book does not mean those faculty have the time or the interest to read it. She had merely picked books she liked and designed a program she would enjoy and would have enjoyed in her first years of teaching. She found how easy it was for new faculty to wonder if there was a party line or administrative agenda lying behind book selection.

She also suspected that a college venue for the program was a bit stifling to free discourse and comfortable conversation. When the Dean of the Chapel, himself new to the college and part of the mentoring program, offered the hospitality of his home, the atmosphere improved. After the first year, spouses of new faculty were included in the general invitation. There were potluck desserts with childcare provided. The design went from what she thought new faculty would want to what they actually needed.

The first several chapters of this book have given an overview of the nature and point of mentoring for new faculty in church-related colleges. This chapter will help you think about how those general aims apply to your particular institution. Your institution's own goals for mentoring will determine the optimal program design for your institution. Once you have designed a program, you will need to recruit suitable mentors and give them good training. This chapter deals with these nuts-and-bolts issues and will be helpful whether you are designing a program from scratch or seeking to improve an existing program.

Setting Goals and Priorities
for Your Particular Mentoring Program

The general goals of mentoring for mission are to pass on the story of the institution's church-related mission and to enhance each faculty member's ability to contribute in his or her own way to that mission. Within these general goals, your institution may have more specific goals and priorities. These more specific goals should influence program design so that the mentoring program at your institution fits your particular needs and those of your new faculty. In reflecting on your specific goals, it is helpful to think through what type of church-related college your institution aspires to be. This will involve thinking hard about the topic discussed in Chapter Two ("All Mentoring Is Local") and applying what you have clarified about the nature of your institution to the area of program design.

In Chapter Two we discussed classifying institutions into six types: Purist Denominational, Purist Evangelical, Purist Ecumenical, Critical Mass Denominational, Critical Mass Ecumenical, and Pluralist. We also looked at some specific examples of Purist and Critical Mass institutions. The goals and priorities of your mentoring program will, at least in part, be shaped by which of these categories your institution occupies, because that will influence your institution's expectations of its faculty members. In many cases, the goals and priorities of your mentoring program will also be influenced by the particular founding religious tradition of your school.

In a Critical Mass institution, especially if it is focused in maintaining not just a Christian but a denominational connection, faculty orientation and mentoring may have as one of its goals informing new faculty about the founding tradition of the institution. This may not be a goal of mentoring programs at Purist Denominational schools, because if all new faculty are required to be members of the founding denomination, they might be assumed to already be informed about denominational distinctives. Intentionally Pluralist schools may also not see informing new faculty about the founding tradition as an important part of mentoring, because such institutions may not value "privileging" the voice of the founding tradition in the conversations that shape the ethos of the college or university. Purist Evangelical schools may identify specific skills and abilities connected to the doctrinal basis of their institution that they aspire to have all faculty members possess. For example, faculty may be required to write a statement of how their teaching and scholarship are informed by Christianity as embodied in the faith statement of the college or university. At institutions where this is the case, mentoring programs should include elements that would aid new faculty in successfully meeting this requirement.

Sitting down with a committee charged with designing or improving your mentoring program and writing lists of features under the following categories will be a helpful exercise:

(1) Salient Features of This Institution

(2) Challenges Faced or Skills and Knowledge Needed by Our Faculty

(3) Goals and Priorities of Our Mentoring Program

Items in category (2) should grow out of what is listed in category (1); category (3), your goals and priorities, should grow out of what is listed in category (2). In this way, the goals and priorities of your particular program will have important connections to the mission and ethos of your particular institution.

Now we will consider three hypothetical colleges with differing salient features and how these differences might shape different goals and priorities for each of the institution's mentoring programs.

As these simplified examples illustrate, well-designed mentoring programs are likely to have some features in common (for example, a method for helping new faculty understand the students at their new home institution) but will also vary in their emphases as a function of their differing histories, situations, and priorities. College B and College C need to help faculty come to terms with more heterogeneity than College A; College C focuses on service learning while College B concentrates on student-faculty research.

College A		
(1) Salient Features of This Institution	(2) Challenges Faced or Skills and Knowledge Needed by Our Faculty	(3) Goals and Priorities of Our Mentoring Program
• Student body made up of primarily first-generation college students. • Emphasis on "value added education." • Purist Evangelical. • Emphasis on integration of faith and learning. • Emphasis on service learning.	CHALLENGES: • "Careerism" among students and parents of students. • Some students may need extra help with acquiring study and writing skills. NEEDED SKILLS AND KNOWLEDGE: • Ability to be articulate about the relevance of faith issues to academic subjects. • Ability to articulate how the Christian life involves active service to others.	• Cultivate understanding of particular student profile and student needs among new faculty. • Improve teaching skills aimed at taking students from where they are to mastery of the subject. • Aid new faculty in becoming fully articulate about the implications of their own faith and the faith statement of the college for their particular discipline.

College B		
(1) Salient Features of This Institution	(2) Challenges Faced or Skills and Knowledge Needed by Our Faculty	(3) Goals and Priorities of Our Mentoring Program
• Student body made up of a mix of Christians and non-Christians. • Emphasis on effective teaching and student-faculty research • Purist Ecumenical. • Desire to remain faithful in some sense to the college's founding tradition.	CHALLENGES: • Some tensions among students who have firmly held religious views and some non-religious students. • Perceived pressure to achieve high student evaluation scores. NEEDED SKILLS AND KNOWLEDGE: • Familiarity with founding tradition of the college. • Ability to interact with students and colleagues from a variety of faith traditions or (in the case of students) from no faith tradition.	• Cultivate understanding of particular student profile and student needs among new faculty. • Improve teaching skills with emphasis on creative student research opportunities. • Inform new faculty about the founding tradition of the college. • Aid new faculty in becoming comfortable with ecumenical dialogue.

College C		
(1) Salient Features of This Institution	(2) Challenges Faced or Skills and Knowledge Needed by Our Faculty	(3) Goals and Priorities of Our Mentoring Program
• Student body made up of a mix of Christians and non-Christians. • Emphasis on effective teaching and service learning. • Critical Mass Denominational. • Desire to remain faithful to the college's founding tradition.	CHALLENGES: • Some tensions among students and faculty who have firmly held religious views and some non-religious faculty and students. • Perceived tension between time needed for teaching and time needed to design and execute service projects. NEEDED SKILLS AND KNOWLEDGE: • Familiarity with founding tradition of the college and ability to articulate its relationship to service. • Ability to interact well with people of different faiths or no faith.	• Cultivate understanding of particular student profile and student needs among new faculty. • Cultivate dialogue among faculty about faith differences. • Improve teaching skills with emphasis on creative service learning opportunities. • Inform new faculty about the founding tradition of the college. • Aid new faculty in becoming comfortable with ecumenical dialogue.

The founding tradition of an institution can also influence mentoring in more pervasive ways. For example, at one of our schools, St. Peter's Preparatory, founded in the Jesuit tradition, it was natural to root occasions connected with mentoring in the traditional practice of *lectio divinitas*. In this ancient exercise of meditatively reading a text aloud, wisdom is sought by reading and reflecting together while drawing from within that which gives life. In this spirit, a group of six mentoring pairs, colleagues ranging in experience from one to thirty years, accepted the invitation to gather for a *"lectio"* on Parker Palmer's *The Courage to Teach.* This was a community reading of compelling selections from Palmer's book, followed by an engaging reflection on the participants' teaching experiences in light of Palmer's insights. Each found in the reading courage to talk with and listen to each other. They met not as educators are inclined to, focusing on methods, materials, technique, or advances in their respective fields of inquiry. Reading together encouraged them to name the fears that teachers have and also to discern what is life giving and redemptive in the vocation of teaching. They left with the sense that Palmer had helped them see God in all things and nurture the academic virtues of mind and spirit that, when practiced, also open spaces for students to discover life in higher learning.

This is just one example of a creative appropriation of an institution's founding tradition in the service of being a mentoring community. Perhaps such a *lectio* would not fit your institution, given its tradition and ethos. What creative ways can you use to tap into your own institution's rich traditions?

The question of whether your mentoring program will include non-tenure-track faculty is another issue connected with priorities and program design. Many institutions have a considerable number of part-time and adjunct faculty, as well as faculty on one- or two-year contracts. While we have emphasized that mentoring in a Christian context should go beyond directions about how to use the copy machine and obtain a parking permit, many adjuncts and part-time faculty wish that someone had oriented them to even this minimal extent. Christian colleges and universities should be treating their non-tenure-track faculty at least as well as Jesus treated the Syrophoenician woman who pointed out that even the dogs under the table eat the children's crumbs (Mark 7:24-30)! Including non-tenure-track faculty in your regular mentoring program may present challenges for scheduling and compensation, yet given that many part-time and adjunct faculty teach multiple classes for several years, they need to be given some sense of the mission to which their teaching contributes as well as the care and hospitality evidenced in providing basic information. The students they will teach deserve to be given instruction that is as high a quality and as relevant to the mission as students in courses taught by faculty on regular appointments. Institutions with departments that use many non-tenure-track faculty would be wise to consider urging department chairs to find creative ways to provide a modified version of the mentoring program provided for those on tenure track.

The Importance of "Safe Space" in Faculty Mentoring

Whatever your mentoring program's goals and priorities, creating "safe space" for growth should be among them. Any kind of growth involves risk, and new faculty members are more likely to take risks in an environment that allows for a few failures.

A few years ago, one of us who was functioning as a director of mentoring heard a complaint from a senior student, a student who did not generally complain about faculty. The student knew the teacher was new and eager, but was also having difficulty communicating with the class. The director of mentoring knew the problem was not primarily with the new teacher, but a failure in mentoring. The departmental mentor was too busy with his own research to know how his new colleague was doing. The director of mentoring called the department chair and made a request for a new mentor. The chair readily agreed. The new mentor sat in on two sections of the same class and helped the new faculty member think about strategies for improving student learning.

The new colleague was most grateful and a new relationship grew between these two colleagues. The class also profited by a shift in pedagogy. But the crux of the issue for the new colleague came after months of stewing. Would this one problem-and-rescue in the classroom be a black mark in his file? Would he be seen as a bad teacher in an institution that valued teaching above all enterprises? Finally, he acknowledged his greatest worry to the director of mentoring: his discipline had so few appointments nationwide that failure to be tenured at one institution meant he would never teach again anywhere. It had been twenty years since the director of mentoring had thought about that fear: the failure to be tenured, the loss of a job. And yet, she reassured the new colleague, the failure was the institution's for not having provided better mentoring in the first place. Someone who had listened earlier or observed the teaching earlier would have been able to guide more effectively from the outset.

Mentoring programs seek to encourage new faculty to work on their gifts, recognizing their personal imperfections, but also realizing there is no absolute model teacher that one must become in a certain number of years. In designing your mentoring program, you will want to think about what sorts of policies can create "safe space" for problem solving and growth. What sorts of understandings will there be about confidentiality between mentors and the new faculty whom they are mentoring? Can mentoring take place within departments without running afoul of power issues? How will evaluation for growth be kept separate from evaluation for raises and retention, tenure and promotion purposes? Some mentoring programs would rather err on the side of caution, assigning mentors from outside the new person's department and asking that mentors refrain from writing letters for promotion files. Other mentoring programs value what junior faculty can learn from a mentor within their department too much to forego such arrangements unless there are particular problems within a department that would necessitate doing so. Still others have multiple mentors with varying functions: a departmental mentor and a "social" mentor from outside the new faculty person's department. It is important to think about what choices seem most suited to your school situation.

Whatever decision is made should not exclude some roles for administrators as resource people within your mentoring program. Having the provost, dean, or academic vice president of your institution make a presentation on a defining issue to a group meeting of mentors and new faculty can be an effective means of new faculty receiving insight into their institution. Providing settings such as receptions and meals for informal interaction among new faculty and student development staff as well as academic administrators can help with comfort, familiarity, and knowing whom to contact in specific situations.

Identifying Areas for Mentoring
and Thinking about Program Design

The goals and priorities that you have identified for your mentoring program will point to broad areas of growth that you seek for your new faculty. The next question to ask in designing your program concerns effective means to achieving these goals.

What means will you use, for example, to address a goal of helping new faculty become effective teachers? Many institutions have found microteaching workshops and videotaping of new faculty teaching useful in discussing improvement in presentation and discussion leading. Classroom visits by the mentor and the new faculty member to each other's classrooms can foster discussion that will lead to ideas about improving teaching effectiveness.

It is also clear that to direct a mentoring program takes expertise; one must be able to work with, motivate, match, and empower faculty, be detail oriented, and have some knowledge of evaluation.

— End-of-year report from a mentoring director

A common priority of mentoring for mission will be introducing new faculty members to the history of the institution, its founding tradition, and its current ethos. There are various ways that this can be done, and you should make choices on the basis of a judicious understanding of faculty culture at your particular institution. One common strategy involves discussion of a set of common readings. These discussions could take place between mentoring pairs or in group settings. There are several books in the bibliography of this volume that can be useful for discussion of church-related higher education or how particular branches of the Christian faith have shaped their intellectual traditions. Short documents, including your college's mission statement and descriptions from your college catalogue or faculty handbook, can also be very useful foci for discussion. Our experience has taught us that long reading assignments are less successful than short readings, given the heavy demands on faculty time in their normal duties. Panel discussions on topics related to history and mission are also wonderful opportunities for conveying information and stimulating discussion.

This kind of strategic thinking is well illustrated by the mentoring program at one of our home institutions, Midland Lutheran College

(MLC). MLC emphasizes student-centered teaching. This emphasis has generated two particular design features of their mentoring program: a plenary session in which new faculty are presented with relevant information about the student body, and a program of classroom visitation. Meetings between mentors and new faculty during the first few months often center on teaching effectiveness and classroom management, conversations stemming from classroom visitations.

Another feature of MLC's emphasis on teaching is a formal program on putting together a teaching portfolio for promotion and tenure documentation. This program is provided for new faculty during the first semester of each academic year. Mentors are encouraged to help new faculty put together the strongest possible portfolio in order to document their teaching effectiveness.

In addition to these teaching-centered aspects of mentoring, MLC also seeks to help new faculty meet important people on campus and understand how to access resources. Some of the MLC mentors host an open house prior to the beginning of the academic year to introduce new faculty to key people such as the faculty chairperson, head librarian, audiovisual coordinator, and student services counselors. The printed mentor manual and local computer blackboard page at MLC also contain pictures of key persons on campus along with their contact information.

MLC's program works well because they have designed it to address their particular goals. By thinking strategically about your program's design, you can enhance the effectiveness of your own institution's mentoring program.

Group Mentoring and Individual Mentoring

One strategic decision that those designing mentoring programs need to think through is whether to mentor each year's cohort of new faculty as a group, to set up a program of one-to-one mentoring, or to have a mix of group and one-to-one mentoring activities. Both cohort mentoring and one-to-one mentoring have advantages to offer.

One advantage of cohort mentoring is efficiency. The director of the mentoring program can spend his or her energies in setting up a series of group activities throughout the year. The director's duties will consist in either planning and facilitating presentation/discussion sessions or recruiting a relatively small number of presenter/discussion leaders. Because each presentation/discussion benefits multiple participants, cohort mentoring is a very efficient use of staff time.

Another advantage of cohort mentoring is the sense of community that it can engender within the cohort. By attending many activities together throughout the year, each year's cohort of new faculty will come to know one another quite well. Some institutions have chosen to extend group mentoring opportunities to include a mix of faculty and administrative staff. This is one way of extending the sense of community within the campus community, countering the tendency of faculty to have little conception of what, for example, student development staff really do, and vice versa.

One-on-one mentoring is more labor intensive than cohort mentoring, but it has advantages of its own. In facilitating a program that focuses on one-to-one mentoring, the director of mentoring will need to recruit, train, and oversee as many mentors in any given year as there are new faculty being mentored. Each mentor will spend considerable time in mentoring — in conversation and shared activities with the new faculty member and perhaps in classroom observation. Staffing hours, including the hours expended by the mentoring director and all the individual mentors, are likely to be considerably more than the staffing hours needed for cohort mentoring. Yet individual attention provided by one-on-one mentoring provides flexibility, builds significant trust between senior and junior faculty members, and can address the individual needs of each new faculty person.

Many programs combine elements of cohort mentoring and one-on-one mentoring. Group sessions can be used to convey information all new faculty members need, and they can spark general discussion of the institution's history, mission, ethos, and priorities. If both members of each mentoring pair attend group sessions, mentors can engage in follow-up conversations with new faculty members about topics of special interest to individual faculty. Group discussion at such gatherings will provide an opportunity for new faculty to share their questions and opinions and also hear various points of view from senior faculty members. At the same time, mentoring pairs can address particular needs of each new faculty person, perhaps discussing issues that never come up in group sessions.

Such "mixed" programs have several advantages. At institutions that offer one-on-one mentoring, some new faculty may not want an individual mentor, especially one who is assigned to them. Having a program that has both group and one-on-one elements would open the possibility of allowing such faculty to participate in the group sessions but not have an assigned mentor. In other cases, a new faculty member who did want a mentor might be in a particular mentoring pair that is not "clicking" for any number of reasons. As we will discuss more fully in Chapter Five, the mentoring director will want to do his or her best to provide a positive experience to a new faculty person in such a situation, perhaps by troubleshooting with the mentor or in some cases replacing the mentor. Having some sessions that are group-oriented is a way of ensuring in the interim that even if the one-on-one mentoring experience of a particular new faculty person is less than optimal, the larger mentoring community is still caring for him.

Considering the Pros and Cons
of Mandatory Participation

Another decision to be made in designing a mentoring program is whether to make participation mandatory for new faculty members, in all or some of its aspects. Institutions must weigh the pros and cons in their own case and use their own judgment about what is best.

One advantage of mandatory participation is that it guarantees all the members of a new faculty cohort the same kind of introduction to the campus community. A well-planned program will be well worth the new faculty member's time; if an individual faculty member chooses not to participate, that person would be missing a valuable experience. A new faculty member who does not participate in a program that other members of his cohort are having will not only miss out on valuable information and training, but will be isolated to some extent from his colleagues. New faculty members often feel so vividly all the urgent demands on their time that they might forego something billed as "optional" even if they thought that it would be of value. Thus, in some ways making the program mandatory is a way of giving them permission to use their time in this way.

The problem with mandatory participation is that some people, especially faculty members, tend to take a negative attitude toward things that they are required to do. Gerald Gibson, in his book *Good Start: A Guidebook for New Faculty in Liberal Arts Colleges*, characterizes faculty as original thinkers with lots of drive who work most effectively when they genuinely believe in what they are doing. In work they consider valuable, they will organize themselves and see their projects through. Yet because they are self-directed, Gibson observes that they are also people who "can never be driven, [and can] seldom be led" (170). One of the challenges facing any program of faculty development, including mentoring programs, is that it is very difficult to make faculty members do anything they do not personally see value in. You may require them to participate even if they do not recognize the value of the event or program, but you cannot make unconvinced faculty participate in a way that will be effective toward your goals in faculty development. Especially in the case of something as personal as a one-on-one mentoring relationship, required participation might feel like an intrusion. If a new faculty member starts with these negative attitudes, even the best of mentors and the most artfully designed group experiences may have a difficult time winning her over.

One solution that balances both the pros and cons of mandatory participation is to require some parts of the mentoring program for new faculty but make other parts optional. Consider a structure that begins with two to five days of intensive introduction to the institution before classes start during the first year and also includes a series of meetings throughout the year as well as an invitation to be part of a mentoring pair. Such a program might require the pre-college portion while recommending but not requiring the other elements. Designing the optional elements so that they are not just worthwhile but fun and revitalizing will help ensure that voluntary participation is high.

If your program addresses multiple audiences, whether and which parts of the programs are mandatory might vary depending on the audience. Will those on term contracts be invited to participate in your mentoring program along with tenure-track faculty? Will they be required to participate in all aspects of it? Your answers to these questions will depend on whether your goals and priorities apply with equal relevance to both a temporary and tenure-track audience.

Addressing Budgetary and Administrative Issues

One important decision about the structure of a mentoring program concerns the role of the overseer of the program. One former director of mentoring, in reflecting on his experience, told us, "It is clear that to direct a mentoring program takes expertise; one must be able to work with, motivate, match, and empower faculty, be detail oriented, and have some knowledge of evaluation." The quality of the mentoring director can make or break a mentoring program. At many institutions, a mentoring director is recruited from among the senior faculty. In such cases, the person should not only have the abilities to design, execute, evaluate, and improve a good program, but also be widely trusted and respected among faculty colleagues. At some institutions, the director of mentoring role is incorporated into the job description of an appropriate member of the administration. This can work well when the institutional ethos does not set up too many barriers between faculty and administration. At institutions where there is too much distrust between faculty and "the administration" it might be more important for the director of mentoring to be a member of the teaching faculty. One former mentoring director noted tensions caused for her role when she temporarily shifted from being a teaching faculty member to being interim dean for faculty development: "I was acutely aware that, for a couple of people involved in the mentoring program, I had moved from respected faculty member to suspect administrator."

One budgetary consideration when setting up a mentoring program is how the director of mentoring will be compensated. If the role of director of mentoring is part of the job description of someone with an administrative appointment, this may be a non-issue. However, for directors of mentoring appointed from among the faculty, it is appropriate either to give them adequate release time to perform their duties or to pay them a supplementary stipend for work that goes beyond their normal duties.

Varying with campus ethos, expected time commitment, and available funding, some institutions provide stipends for participation to mentors, to new faculty, or to both. Stipends are usually seen as a way of acknowledging the value of faculty time and the importance that the institution places on this use of it. Stipends are usually modest ($200 to $500 for the year) but considered to be significant symbols. Some programs simply give gift certificates to mentors in lieu of stipends. Some institutions with very ambitious mentoring programs grant new faculty a reduced teaching load because they are expected to participate in a weekly faculty seminar with a hefty reading list and writing assignments. Other institutions have found that both mentors and new faculty members do not need extra incentives to participate and are happy to be a part of the program for its intrinsic value.

Discretionary funds to support mentoring activities can be valuable. At Abilene Christian University, each mentor was given a two-hundred-dollar discretionary budget for social activities with his or her new faculty member. Some used this for taking the new faculty person and spouse to dinner or a cultural event; one mentor enrolled himself and his new faculty member in the same health club, where they had useful conversations while working out together. On a somewhat smaller scale, mentors at Hope College were invited to take their new faculty members out to lunch once a semester and be reimbursed for up to twenty-five dollars.

Another budgetary item to be considered is funds to supply food and hospitality for group events. Many programs combine group discussions and panel presentation with lunch or dinner either on campus or at a nearby restaurant. Breaking bread together is an important aspect of being a mentoring community and is well worth the modest costs involved.

Other potential budget items are honoraria for guest speakers, costs of books to be provided to mentors and new faculty, and photocopying and other material costs. Some programs have used small amounts of money in creative ways to honor mentors or to add a sense of fun to events. One program had special "mentoring mugs" made to present to mentors. Another program furnished door prizes consisting of college logo items at group events. Programs that have group events to which spouses are invited would be wise to invest in the cost of furnishing childcare, so that faculty with young children will not be deterred from attendance. Total budgets for mentoring programs of which we are aware vary from $2000 to $10,000, not counting such hidden costs as release time for mentoring directors. It has often been noted that one can tell quite a bit about what a person really values by looking at his or her desk calendar, checkbook, and credit card statements. In the same way, how much an institution expends and in what concrete ways it fosters a mentoring community demonstrate institutional priorities.

Identifying and Recruiting Good Mentors

Research shows that new faculty members are able best to work with mentors who are direct, honest, and willing to share their knowledge, allow growth, and give psitive and critical feedback (Knox and McGovern). Mentors act as guides and hosts, welcoming and acquainting the new faculty member with the ethos of his or her new home institution. Mentors should be good listeners, encouragers, and able to maintain confidentiality when appropriate. Mentors can also function as role models and advisors for new faculty.

Goodwin, Stevens, and Bellamy (1998) investigated faculty members' attitudes, perceptions, and experiences about faculty-to-faculty mentoring. They found that elements rated as important to the mentoring relationship were mutual respect, accessibility of the mentor, and a perception that the mentor had volunteered to be a mentor because of genuine care for new faculty members.

Everyone carries with them at least one and probably
Many pieces to someone else's puzzle.
Sometimes they know it.
Sometimes they don't.
And when you present your piece
Which is worthless to you,
To another, whether you know it or not,
Whether they know it or not,
You are a Messenger from the Most High.

— Lawrence Kushner,
Honey from the Rock, 69-70

Because one of the goals of mentoring for mission is helping each new faculty member fully own and contribute in his or her own way to the mission of the college, mentors should be people who have a genuine appreciation for their institution's mission. Yet those who are recruited to be mentors do not necessarily need to know everything about the institution in order to be a good candidate. Nor, as we noted earlier, do mentors at Critical Mass or Pluralist institutions necessarily need to be Christians in order to be fully committed to the mission of the college and possess the virtues requisite for mentoring.

How does a dean, director of faculty development, or facilitator of a mentoring program, discern those with mentoring gifts? Observation is likely to reveal who the likely candidates for mentors are at your institution. Who do people naturally go to for advice? Who is widely respected and trusted? Your personal observations can be supplemented by those of others; often it is desirable to ask department chairs and chairs of committees for suggestions of good potential mentors. Many institutions have recruited some of their mentors from among emeritus faculty members. Often emeritus faculty members have a wealth of wisdom and experience to share and are happy to have a continuing contribution to the institution.

One challenge to be faced in recruiting mentors from among current senior faculty is that those who have the qualities for mentoring are likely to have been elected or appointed to college-wide committees and other tasks that need gifted and trustworthy people. With so many other demands on their time, will they be willing to make one more time-consuming commitment?

Be wary of senior faculty who have demonstrated a desire to pontificate in their relations with junior faculty in the past. While the mentor and mentee are clearly differentiated by experience, the relationship should be that of friends and essentially equals.

— End-of-year report from a mentoring director

Another incentive to becoming a mentor can be the personal touch. At one of our home institutions, the director of mentoring spent considerable time interviewing each new faculty member to see what he or she wanted out of the mentoring relationship and what traits were especially valued in a mentor. One new faculty person was especially looking for help in setting up a research agenda; another wanted to learn how to create enthusiasm in initially resistant students; yet another wanted a role model for deftly balancing family and professional responsibilities. The director of mentoring then sat down and reflected on who she knew among her senior colleagues who had the traits that each new faculty member seemed to need in a mentor. When asking a senior faculty person to consider being a mentor, she was able to tell the person, "You would be perfect for mentoring so-and-so; you are just the kind of strong classroom teacher (or researcher or balanced contributor) he (or she) wants and needs in a mentor." Such a personal "call" is a strong incentive for a positive response.

In recruiting mentors, it is also helpful to point out that being a mentor is not totally self-sacrificial. A byproduct of being a mentor is learning from those who are being mentored. When recruiting mentors, it helps to emphasize the intrinsic rewards of contributing to the well-being of another person and the honor in being asked to fulfill this important role.

Mentoring Mentors

As Shulamith Reich Elster observes, "One can have a green thumb for relationships as well as for gardening" (58). Of course, training and structured programs make inherently good mentors even better.

At Hope College, where one of the emphases is on mentors visiting new faculty in the classroom, mentors are invited to an initial session in which they observe role-plays of discussions of syllabi and debriefing after classroom observation. Mentors then pair up and take turns giving helpful feedback. People are asked to practice such skills as finding strengths to praise while also noting areas for growth. New faculty members are also asked to fill out a questionnaire about their preferences for receiving feedback, which are then given to each mentor as background information.

In addition to helping mentors hone good listening and modeling skills, mentors must be trained in the history, tradition, and needs of their own institutions. Mentors do not just explain how the new teacher goes about finding a copying machine and applying for faculty development grants; they also model an awareness and appreciation of the mission and the values underlying membership in the college community. This means that experienced faculty members need to have opportunities to discuss their role and the role of the mission in the life of the college with each other and with new faculty members.

The power of heritage, its ability to inspire and motivate — or to constrain — is indisputable. The faculty who have weathered together the ebb and flow of institutional trial and achievement, share a sense of what matters and how things are done.

— Gerald Gibson,
Good Start, p. 57

As we have emphasized earlier in this chapter, mission-based aspects of men-

86

toring will vary with nuances in the respective missions of institutions. The Weyerhauser Center for Faith and Learning at Whitworth College, for example, has sponsored workshops over the past few years to instruct its faculty in its own Reformed tradition, but also to educate faculty in the various traditions from which its faculty come. A workshop in the summer of 2001 invited participants to prepare materials from their church traditions — Roman Catholic, Methodist, Quaker, Anglican, and Baptist, for example — related to a series of common questions, including the issue of calling or vocation. The Whitworth program was not restricted to those who had been recruited as mentors; nevertheless, as potential mentors these faculty have been given tools to aid those they are called to serve.

Another example: the University of Scranton, a Jesuit institution with a desire to ensure that more faculty understand how the Jesuit tradition contributes to pedagogy, made this the focus of its 1999-2000 Lilly Foundation Mentoring Grant. By having potential mentors take a "pre-test" on what the institution thought was central to an understanding of Jesuit pedagogy, the directors of the mentoring program were able to identify areas in which the mentors needed additional information and training. Sessions for mentors were designed to give mentors a fuller grasp of the Jesuit tradition. These twenty mentors then shared with twenty newer colleagues in learning together the implications of this instruction. This process is one of the ways mentors may not only learn about the tradition of the institution but also pass it on to others.

Mentors who participate in group discussions of how mentoring relates to mission are likely to be more comfortable and better equipped in addressing these issues with new faculty. Consider having mentors read and discuss together a reading on church-related higher education (many good options are listed in the bibliography of this book). Profitable conversations on mentoring can also be based on having mentors read Chapters One, Two, and Three of this book and discussing them together, as well as the reflection questions for mentors contained in Appendix Two.

Mentoring mentors should go beyond an initial training session. A director of mentoring can often function as a sounding board for mentors as they try to think through how best to help new faculty with particular issues. In one case, a mentor who had been diagnosed with a medical condition requiring considerable time for treatment approached the mentoring director to see if it would be advisable for a new mentor, one who would be less distracted, to be assigned to the new faculty person in question. Conversation with the mentoring director allowed the mentor to see that one of the things the new faculty member, who was trying to cope with a difficult family situation, needed was a model of how to handle the messiness and unpredictability of life. The mentor decided to continue in the mentoring relationship, to the benefit of both the new faculty member and herself. Mentoring and nurturing mentors is a vital aspect of being a healthy mentoring community.

BIBLIOGRAPHY

Elster, Shulamith Reich. "Unimagined Bridges: On Mentors and Proteges." In *Touching the Future: Mentoring and the Jewish Professional,* ed. Michael Zeldin and Sara S. Lee, 56-61. Los Angeles: Rhea Hirsch School of Education, Hebrew Union College-Jewish Institute of Religion, 1995.

Gibson, Gerald W. *Good Start: A Guidebook for New Faculty in Liberal Arts Colleges.* Bolton, MA: Anker Publishing Company, Inc., 1992.

Goodwin, L. D., E. A. Stevens, and G. T. Bellamy. "Mentoring among Faculty in Schools, Colleges and Departments of Education." *Journal of Teacher Education* 49, no. 5 (1998): 334-44.

Knox, Pamela L., and Thomas V. McGovern. "Mentoring Women in Academia." *Teaching of Psychology,* 15, No. 1 (1988): 39-41.

Kushner, Lawrence. *Honey from the Rock: Visions of Jewish Mystical Renewal.* New York: Harper & Row, 1977.

Palmer, Parker. *The Courage to Teach: Exploring the Inner Landscape of a Teacher's Life.* San Francisco: Jossey-Bass, 1998.

CHAPTER FIVE

Facing Challenges and Achieving Lasting Success

What Do You Think I Should Say?

"Do you have a few minutes?" he asked as she passed by his open door and nodded hello.

"Sure. What's up?"

"Well, I'm not sure whether I should be talking to you about this, but I know that you've been a mentor a couple of times and I'm kind of stuck. I'm a mentor for the first time and I went to Sam's class yesterday. I'm not sure what I should do about what I saw."

"Well, I may end up saying, 'I don't know,' but tell me what the problem is."

"I don't think you know Sam, but he has a very 'in your face,' provocative style of teaching. He paces energetically in the front of the

89

room, talking quickly. He asks questions, but only pauses a short time and supplies his own answers to the questions. He doesn't leave much room for students to discuss or respond. Some of his students seem to be responding well to this, looking interested, paying attention. But I was sitting toward the back of the classroom, and I could tell by body language that he is not connecting at all with the back three rows of his class. Only two or three students spoke at all during the whole hour. His teaching style is so different from mine that I'm not sure how to help him. We are supposed to meet tomorrow. What do you think I should say?"

"Hmmmm. That sounds tough. I can tell you the way I'd start, and you can see if it makes sense to you. I tend to ask very open-ended questions to begin: 'How did you feel about the class? What did you most want to get done? Do you think it was accomplished?' That sort of thing. How much I go into detail about my reactions depends on my sense of who I am talking to. If the person I observed seems to have a lack of confidence, I am extremely gentle about making suggestions and try to find several things to praise in what I saw. Sometimes the most important thing to do to improve teaching is to develop self-confidence. In Sam's case, I wonder whether he has *too much* confidence. He may have a strong enough personality that you can be very straight with him about your reactions and observations and he'll debate points with you that he thinks are off base. You could ask him at some point how much he thinks he is holding the attention of the bulk of his students."

"I'll think about it. I'm not looking forward to this very much. What if he gets defensive or even angry? It could be a hard conversation."

Meeting Ethical Challenges

All human activities pose ethical issues, though some of these seem so clear to us that we hardly notice them, taking their solutions for granted. There are always subtle ethical issues inherent in the mentoring relationship, which is why, in Chapter One, we emphasized mentoring as an exercise of virtues.

One recurrent issue is the tension between tact and honesty. If the mentor has made a classroom visit and come away with several concerns about the quality of what she observed, she may feel torn between being frank and being kind. Avoiding all suggestions for improvement would be a false kindness, for the new faculty person desires to become the best teacher she can be. Piling on more suggestions than the person is able to deal with is also unlikely to be helpful. Discernment among issues of personal taste and issues that affect instructional quality is also needed.

Mentors also can have considerable influence over new faculty members and must take care not to use that influence for the mentors' personal gratification or agenda. Mentors who have strong opinions about campus political issues (curriculum reform or nominees for important academic posts, for example) should guard against trying to enlist the new faculty whom they are mentoring onto their "side." Mentors should also avoid paternalism in mentoring; new faculty are new at the institution, but they are adults who need to be treated as such. Mentors should not be overly directive.

Occasionally, mentoring directors and mentors may face more complicated ethical situations. Because "safe space" is an important element of a mentoring program, we have emphasized confidentiality between mentors and new faculty. Conceivably, a mentor might find herself in a situation where disclosures within the mentoring relationship reveal serious problems. Perhaps the new faculty person has violated a regulation of the university or college; perhaps the new faculty person is struggling with clinical depression and is having real difficulty fulfilling contractual duties; perhaps the new faculty person is being subjected to sexual harassment. What should a mentor do in such situations?

Recipes obviously cannot be given at a general level for all conceivable situations, but there are relevant general principles. First, the mentor is primarily a source of counsel. The first strategy to use in almost all situations is to seek to lead the new faculty member to take active responsibility for the situation. If this strategy is successful, the mentor will not have to consider whether to intervene more actively. The mentor should urge the person who has violated a college regulation to confess and make reparations. She should urge the depressed faculty member to seek professional help and to be frank with his immediate supervisor. She should urge the new faculty person who is being sexually harassed to take the steps that are appropriate through the campus sexual harassment policy. In some situations, it would be appropriate for the mentor to offer to be present during difficult conversations in order to provide moral support.

If the strategy of helping the new faculty member take personal responsibility is unsuccessful, the responsibilities of the mentor may have come to an end, at least in many situations. The advantage of having a mentoring program that distinguishes mentoring from supervisory relationships is that supervision is still being given and is clearly someone else's responsibility. If a new faculty member is not fulfilling his contractual duties, this will come to light without the mentor "reporting" on the new faculty member. Mentors may from time to time be asked to comment on their impressions of the quality of new faculty teaching. In such situations, a gentle reminder that the mentoring relationship is confidential would be appropriate. This needs to be the uniform response whether the teaching evaluation would be positive or negative, lest a plea of confidentiality be interpreted as a negative report.

If serious, ongoing harms become apparent to the mentor, the need to prevent future harm can overrule obligations of confidentiality. If a new faculty member, for example, revealed that he was having an affair with a student and would neither desist nor confess this to his chair or dean, the mentor should strongly consider reporting the situation. Out of respect for the mentoring relationship, if the mentor finds himself in such a situation, he should explain to the new faculty member that he intends to make the disclosure, to whom, and why. Blessedly, such situations are rare.

Never Enough Time

Perhaps the most common recurring concern of those involved in planning and overseeing mentoring is time. New faculty may feel that they just do not have the time to come to group discussions or meet with their mentor one on one. When senior faculty members are asked to function as mentors, some decline, regretting that they "just don't have the time." Some who make commitments to be mentors end up neglecting their duties to their new faculty members because other time commitments crowd out the time that they would spend mentoring. Course preparation, grading, interaction with students, departmental and committee duties, research time, even time to get adequate sleep, seem to crowd one another out already without adding yet one more commitment. Mentoring can seem like one item too many on a painfully overloaded agenda.

The problem of time needs to be addressed at both spiritual and practical levels. Complaints of a lack of time or a coveting of time often reveal how impoverished we think we are. Too often faculty and administrators think that time is an empty space quickly filled with meetings for departments, divisions, colleges, universities, disciplines, classes, research, and writing. Yet within the Christian tradition, stewardship does not look at the universe, life, and time as limited resources for which we must compete. In many branches of Christianity, liturgical calendars, emphasizing the rhythm of the church year, remind us that Christians can envision time differently: not as a crowded space in which to shoehorn one more activity but as the gracious provision of a generous God. Mentoring can call us to cultivate a Christian sense of time, affecting how we receive it, use it, and spend it. When a generous, gracious spirit fashions time, we can act in faith that God will not stint on giving us time for hospitality, care, communion, and nurture. The disciples in the gospel narratives of the feedings of multitudes needed to learn that when people genuinely care for the needs of others, God will provide enough and more than enough. In a similar way, we need to believe that God will honor our desires to embody a mentoring community by providing enough time.

There are also some practical considerations that can help people make time for mentoring and being mentored. Some institutions are so convinced that their programs for new faculty are of vital importance that they provide release time for participants and for those who have major staffing responsibilities connected to the program. Other schools structure group aspects of mentoring programs as one-, two-, or three-week summer seminars with stipends provided for participation.

Many college and university administrators do not believe their institutional realities allow for these relatively expensive options. In such cases, group aspects of their programs are likely to be built around a lunch or dinner hour. Forethought and strategic planning can avoid common pitfalls of this sort of programming. Many lunch programs for faculty have foundered on the complication of not being able to find even one time slot in weekly schedules that works for all potential participants. One way of solving this problem is to ask chairs of all new faculty to refrain from scheduling their new faculty members in what will be understood to be the "mentoring slot" for a given year. If mentors as well as new faculty are to be invited to group sessions, senior faculty who have agreed to act as mentors for the coming semester should be informed of what the "mentoring slot" is and be asked to guard it in their schedules. In some institutions, junior faculty, including new faculty, are often asked to teach evening courses. If this is the case at your institution and your mentoring program is to be built around dinner meetings, you could use this same strategy of a "mentoring slot" to avoid conflicts with new faculty evening teaching duties. If such pre-planning seems unworkable at your institution, one fallback strategy would involve asking everyone at the beginning of the semester to submit their schedule to the person planning meetings and for that person to seek to find a slot that maximizes the possibility of attendance among potential participants.

Sometimes it can seem that there is "never enough time" because mentoring directors and mentors have more and more things put on their agendas by others who would like to have tasks done. In such situations, it is important to have a clear sense of boundaries for your mentoring program, so that a polite "no" can be a response to requests that go beyond what mentoring means at your institution. The best way to have clear boundaries is to have thought clearly about your program's nature, goals, and priorities, as we discussed in Chapter Four. Would it be appropriate for your mentoring program to become the mechanism for recruiting and training of faculty for the first-year seminar program? Would it be appropriate for the mentoring director to be the contact person for getting office keys and faculty parking stickers? These questions are best addressed within the context of a clear sense of the main purposes of your particular institution's program.

For one-on-one mentoring pairs who are having difficulties getting together, time can often be "stretched" for both members of a mentoring pair by combining conversation with another activity. Mentoring over lunch is an obvious example, but there are others. We all need exercise, and many mentoring pairs have important exchanges while sitting side by side on exercise bikes, while playing racquetball, or while jogging or walking together.

It is also considerate to take into account potential childcare needs of new faculty members, especially for activities to which spouses are invited. Inviting spouses to social events for new faculty and even to some content sessions can help give them a sense of ownership and understanding of the college or university. Young faculty may view a dinner meeting as less "costly" in its effects on their family time if their spouses are included. Even if spouses are not invited, some new faculty members can be faced with the choice of caring for their child or attending the mentoring event. Providing childcare means they do not have to make that choice.

One last practical consideration with regard to time is that people will usually make time for what they find to be important, valuable, and enjoyable. Well-planned events that assure people that their time will be well spent will sustain an audience. Thinking of things that can also make those events fun occasions — meeting at a nice restaurant if the budget allows for that, having a pleasant dinner in someone's home, or providing door prizes for on-campus events — can be an aspect of the hospitality of the mentoring community.

Cultivating Ownership
without Creating an "Inner Circle"

Mentoring for Christian mission naturally holds up role models of what the college values in its faculty. Mentoring often seeks to cultivate certain attitudes, skills, and understanding among new faculty. Depending on the "demographics of ownership" (discussed in Chapter Two), senior faculty at some institutions who are not a part of the mentoring program may misconstrue the nature of mentoring for mission, seeing it as signaling the fact that the institution has an "inner circle" of preferred faculty members, of which they are not a part. In some departments in some institutions, this may lead senior faculty to raise suspicions among junior members about the "hidden agenda" of the mentoring program, leading new faculty to fear being indoctrinated if they participate.

It is difficult to guard against all the potential ill effects of misinformation and unfounded suspicion. However, one can think carefully about design features of a mentoring program that can undermine the perception that there is some "inner circle" of power and prestige that the program aspires to perpetuate.

One way of doing this is in the careful selection of mentors and program personnel. Mentors can be selected who have strengths for the position but also so that the pool of mentors represents a wide circle of faculty. What this "wide circle" looks like will vary depending on whether the institution is Purist, Critical Mass, or Pluralist. At a Purist institution that hires only members of the college's founding tradition or those who can ascribe to the same statement of faith, "a wide circle of faculty" may designate those who hold a variety of opinions on matters not definitive of the institution's theological core. At a Denominational Critical Mass school where there is some suspicion that those who are adherents of the founding denomination are part of an inner circle, recruiting some mentors who are not adherents of that tradition may be important. Such mentors can model full contribution to the college's mission on the part of those whose faith commitments are not those of the founders.

Using a panel discussion format for some group sessions connected with mentoring can also help undercut a perception that there is a "party line" that the mentoring program is attempting to foist on new faculty. At Hope College, for example, one dinner meeting for new faculty was entitled "Hope College Then and Now." Four faculty members who were also Hope alumni talked about what the college had seemed like when they were students and the changes they had seen over time. The point of the panel was not to signal that Hope alumni are "privileged" among Hope faculty, but to show that perceptions of the college differed even among people who had that common experience. Though the panelists were all alumni, they were chosen from different generations of students and faculty and were known to differ with one another on their views concerning salient aspects of the college. The panelists also represented various positions on the theological spectrum from liberal to conservative and various denominational affiliations. New faculty learned that not even alumni faculty at Hope College were a homogeneous group and that difference was valued as an institutionally recognized good.

A University is, according to the usual designation, as Alma Mater, knowing her children one by one, not a foundry, or a mint, or a treadmill.

— John Henry Cardinal Newman, *The Idea of a University*, 109

96

Dealing with a Mentoring Relationship
That Is Not Working

One problem that mentoring directors who are overseeing one-on-one mentoring programs may face from time to time is a mentoring relationship that is not working well. Addressing such situations earlier rather than later can help facilitate problem solving. In order to do this, the mentoring director will have to have ways of getting frequent "readings" of how things are going for mentoring pairs. One system that has worked well for some mentoring directors is to send out periodic e-mail messages to both mentors and new faculty providing encouragement, helpful information briefly stated, and ending with "How's it going? Please let me know if there is any way that I can be of help to you." This is a way of reminding both mentors and new faculty that they should be actively involved as a mentoring pair and that the mentoring director is available as a resource.

Problems within mentoring pairs can have various sources. Sometimes a new faculty member will feel the need for more time than the mentor seems willing to provide but may feel unable to express the wish to get together more often. In other instances, there may be a mismatch of personal or professional styles that keeps the mentoring pair from working well together. In some cases, a particular mentor may know the institution so thoroughly that he or she has a hard time anticipating what new faculty will need to be told or will find interesting. In such cases, the mentor may overload the new faculty member with institutional lore or talk in insider lingo that fails to communicate.

A first step for a mentoring director in addressing such situations is an extended conversation with the member of the mentoring pair that perceives the problem. In the best-case scenario, the mentoring director can help with strategies for opening up a conversation between the mentoring partners. Advice that helps the pair iron out differences on their own is preferable to direct involvement on the part of the mentoring director. However, in some cases, the mentoring director may have to invite the other member of the mentoring pair for a conversation. In some cases where new faculty members feel neglected by their mentors, just having the wish for more interaction voiced may be enough to solve the problem. In other cases, a mentor may have overestimated how many commitments she could take on at a given time and

97

may need to ask to be replaced because of lack of time to do an adequate job. Mentors may also need to be replaced if there seems to be a mismatch of personalities, though in some cases interaction with someone significantly different than oneself can be a valuable growth experience. When mentors need to be replaced, care should be taken to do this as diplomatically as possible.

Doing More with Less

Changes in institutional circumstances often result in funding being reduced even to programs that the institution views as valuable. Mentoring programs can experience such reductions and need to be able to deal with them while minimizing adverse effects on new faculty.

Communication is key in making necessary adjustments when budgets are reduced. One sad story that we know of illustrates this well. A mentoring program was begun with the full support of the current president and with some external funding. The president paid each of four initial planners of the program a stipend of $1000 for summer planning from his budget for summer planning. When the mentoring program began they had an ample budget of about 10,000 dollars per year. Stipends of $1000 were paid to mentors, and there were more than adequate funds for materials and meals. After the external funding was gone and a new president with slightly different priorities had come, the director of mentoring attended a budget meeting with the administrative council and was told he would have to make the mentoring program work with a budget of $2000 for the year. Stipends for mentors decreased to $200 per year, meals became less lavish, and other adjustments were made. The following year he was told he had $2500 to work with and the same for the next year. During all of these budget years, the mentoring director never received any bills or account balance sheets from the finance office; he assumed he had balanced the money he had to work with the expenses paid out. However, he later learned that no budget line was ever created, nor were funds put into the existing mentoring budget line.

Consequently, when he called the controller in August to see how much money he had to work with for the coming year he was told that mentoring was over $6000 in the red. Although he was told that monies were in the account, no one saw to it that they were; all of his requests for payment to people and the food service were paid out of the restricted account originally set up for the external funding. The mentoring director was shocked to hear all this, and it took considerable time to clear up, but it was not as bad as it might have been because the dean and president were supportive enough of the mentoring program to cover the "deficit" and to find continuing funds within the dean's budget to continue operations.

Of course, those in charge of mentoring budgets should not overlook the advantages of looking for sources of outside funding. Working with your campus's development department to write grants for enhancing specific aspects of the mentoring program could circumvent the necessity of doing more with less money. Still, as the above example illustrates, mentoring programs can face enormous challenges when grant monies run out. The difference between a challenge and a nightmare can be communication among administrators, the mentoring director, and the business office.

Sometimes having to do more with less can open up creative options. If stipends for mentors need to be reduced or eliminated, a mentoring director should consult with relevant administrators about alternatives to money as a way of signaling the value that the institution places on the willingness to mentor. Many institutions have faculty recognition luncheons or dinners at which those who have had significant publications, or receive grants or external rewards, are asked to stand to receive applause. Having those who have served as faculty mentors in the previous year be included for recognition would be a way of symbolizing that this is also an important professional contribution.

Many faculty members feel that they receive mixed messages from their institutions. When asked to serve the institution in a capacity like mentoring, they are told that this activity is very important. But at evaluation time, "service" may seem to come in a distant third to teaching and scholarly activity in its influence on the size of merit increases. Mentoring is a time-consuming and important activity; especially if it is not supported through stipends, it deserves recognition of its value with appropriate honor at evaluation time.

Programs faced with budget reductions have also, in some cases, found creative ways to stretch food and hospitality budgets. One program that had paid for meals at restaurants or catering on campus replaced these with potluck dinners at someone's home when their budget was reduced. The food was still good and the casual atmosphere generated a sense of community. Some institutions have also found that brown bag lunch discussions draw almost as well as more expensive catered lunches.

The necessity of doing more with less can be the mother of invention. However, it should also be noted that pinching pennies for mentoring may be a false economy from an institutional point of view. If creating ownership of the mission is important, if being gracious to new faculty is an embodiment of Christian hospitality, if helping new faculty hone needed skills and assimilate core values is vital, then mentoring programs are well worth funding. The level of funding should not necessitate those who staff such programs bearing inordinate and uncompensated personal costs, nor should it send a message to new faculty that doing things "on the cheap" is a normal part of their new home institution. In some cases, directors of mentoring may appropriately remind relevant administrators of these "home truths" during budget discussions.

Measuring Effectiveness and Making Improvements

What is the outcome for mentors and those mentored? Can or should these outcomes be measured or assessed? As we will discuss in Chapter Six, at a general level, these questions have already been given positive answers. In their summary of research on mentoring and citing an earlier source, Cheryl and Scott Wright conclude that, in a business setting, having a mentor may result in "increased job satisfaction, higher salary, faster promotion, firmer career plans" and the likelihood that the person being mentored will in turn become a mentor (204). Robert L. Menges's research in *Faculty in New Jobs* revealed that faculty with mentors "had greater success in coping, less social isolation and stress, and better student evaluations than those who were not mentored" (126). But those concerned with mentoring programs will want to know more than that mentoring is generally effective; they will want to know if mentoring is making the differences they want it to make at their institution.

Chapter Four helped you to think about the outcomes that you desire from your particular program. In many cases, evaluation strategies can be aimed at measuring the success of those program objectives, although some care may need to be taken to avoid undermining one objective by measuring another. For example, suppose that one of your objectives is to ensure that new faculty understand some basic aspects of the founding tradition of the institution and how these shape the institution's philosophy of education. Suppose that another objective is creating positive attitudes among new faculty in order to improve faculty retention. One way of measuring how much faculty have learned about the founding tradition would be to test them at the end of the program year, but such a test would be likely to be off-putting rather than to create a positive attitude. A better and more enjoyable way of discerning how much new faculty now know about the founding tradition might be to have a group debriefing at the end of the year that included such questions as: "What do you know now about Catholicism (or Lutheranism or the Reformed or Quaker tradition) that you didn't know when you started here?" "What do you still not understand that it would be helpful to learn?"

Some programs have a seminar format that includes faculty producing a written product or making a presentation at the end of the year. Such activities are of intrinsic value, but reading over them with an eye to what is going well and what could be strengthened in the mentoring program can also be useful for the director of mentoring.

We learned that mentors should be required (rather than encouraged) to submit monthly activity reports so that we could have recognized when a dysfunctional team had sputtered to a halt.

— End-of-year report from a mentoring director

Many programs seek written evaluation from both new faculty members and mentors at least once a year, and in some cases more frequently. Questions can be asked that solicit feedback on particular group sessions, on materials and readings used in the program, and on the value of various aspects of the mentoring experience. Group or individual discussion with new faculty who are "graduating" from the program focusing on what they think might make the program even more valuable to future new faculty is often illuminating. At one of our institutions the mentoring director met with each new faculty member, starting her conversation by saying, "Tell me the story of your year."

Sustaining Energy and Refreshing the Vision

New programs are usually exciting for the people who are designing and implementing them. The people most directly involved have freshly thought through what the program objectives are and how they can best be accomplished. As time goes by, programs must face the challenge of how to sustain energy and vision as the memory of why the goals that the program fosters are crucial becomes dim. Familiarity can take the luster off the vision.

Sometimes programs lose energy by falling into an unexamined routine. A mentor at one institution we know of had been on the faculty for more than a dozen years. She had guarded time in her busy schedule for a mentor training session, but was disappointed to find that discussion at the session revolved around the same handout on leading class discussion that she had been given as a first-year faculty member. Perhaps that handout deserved to be revered as a classic about which she needed to be reminded over and over. She suspected, however, that the person leading the session had had time enough to pull the sheet out of a file folder, but had not taken time recently to read anything fresh about pedagogy or to reflect on any new lessons worth passing on from his own classroom experience. She resented her time being wasted on something with which she was already well acquainted.

Effective mentoring programs can be very labor-intensive for the program coordinator: identifying appropriate mentors, ensuring regular conversations and activities throughout the year, developing appropriate evaluation instruments and processes, scheduling, etc. It is important to anticipate the needed time commitment to the project.

— End-of-year report from a
mentoring director

Perhaps the mentoring director who designed that session was overburdened. A mentoring director who is losing energy for his work may need to take a sabbatical from that specific duty or a formal full sabbatical for at least a semester. Specific term limits for mentoring directors may be worth considering. Yet sometimes what is needed is not replacement, but group support. Forming an advisory committee for your mentoring program can facilitate the evaluation process but can also help ensure that new ideas and fresh energy are continually introduced to the program.

Sometimes what is needed to sustain

the vision of living as a mentoring community is to remind ourselves of where we would be without the robust sense of community that mentoring helps foster. University professor Jane Tompkins, in her memoir *A Life in School*, recalls going through her files one day and finding a note she had made for herself about what she wanted her academic life to be like and where it fell short of those aspirations. That note read, in part:

What I am looking for:
– A common enterprise
– Belonging
– Good feelings in the workplace
– A community of hope
– An integrated life

Why don't these things exist now in the university?
– People are isolated from each other and from themselves
– by their individual interests, professional and personal
– by their departments
– by their crowded time schedules
– by the physical distances between them
– by the psychological distances between them
– by the absence of a culture of conversation
– by a belief that their welfare depends on the work they do in isolation from one another.

How can these obstacles be overcome?
– by a commitment to finding a community of like-minded people
– by a willingness to pay the price in personal advancement and scholarly achievement as these things are measured
– by constructing an alternative reward system. (191-92)

Tompkins goes on to reflect that "[p]eaceable kingdoms aren't born; they are made" (193). We commit the sin of ingratitude if we start taking the progress, however small, that we have made toward being a peaceable kingdom for granted.

When Israel wanted to guard against the sin of ingratitude they communally rehearsed their salvation history. Think of those great psalms of remembrance like Psalms 105 and 106. A mentoring director or mentor may be wise to keep a file of comments from former new faculty who have benefited from the program. Academic culture at large is subject to many forces of fragmentation, as Tompkins's reflections note. At Christian liberal arts colleges and universities we need to fight letting those forces undermine our sense of community and common mission. Just as in the classic film "A Wonderful Life" an ordinary person did not realize how much difference for the good his life was making, so in our hectic lives we may forget that what seems like a pretty ordinary mentoring program can make an immense contribution to community. We need to help one another remember, so that we can be continually refreshed by the vision of generous nurture that originally made us commit ourselves to being a mentoring community.

BIBLIOGRAPHY

Newman, John Henry Cardinal. *The Idea of a University.* New York: Holt, Rinehart & Winston, 1960.

Menges, Robert L., and associates. *Faculty in New Jobs: A Guide to Settling In, Becoming Established, and Building Institutional Support.* San Francisco: Jossey-Bass, 1999.

Tompkins, Jane. *A Life in School: What the Teacher Learned.* Reading, MA: Addison-Wesley, 1996.

Wright, Cheryl A., and Scott D. Wright. "The Role of Mentors in the Career Development of Young Professionals." *Family Relations Journal of Applied Family and Child Studies* 36, no. 2 (1987): 204-8.

CHAPTER SIX

The Bottom Line: Outcomes of Mentoring

- *Avoiding Mixed Signals*
- *Building Ownership of the Mission and Collegiality*
- *Improving Faculty Retention*
- *A Happy Side Effect: Rejuvenating Veteran Faculty and Building Future Leadership*
- *Enhancing Professional Development*
- *Mentoring: A Lamp that Illuminates Other Aspects of the Institution*

Avoiding Mixed Signals

It was a departmental tradition: the grand old historian of religion would take the new colleague on a walking tour of the college town. The historian was a scholar of both the town's and college's cultural history, and the new colleague considered the tour a treat. He was fascinated by the convergence of faith and culture. As they moved between the architectural and horticultural signs of the town's rich ethnic history, the historian commented on the religion department's daring choice to invite the new colleague — a scholar in Catholic studies — to teach at Faith College. The new colleague told his tour guide that he appreciated being at a college where the air was thick with its piety. The tour ended with a jaunt through the east side of town, the burgeoning Hispanic community, and a stop for a coffee, sandwich, and slice of cherry pie at a diner famous for its pies.

The church historian's passion for the town and college were palpable, conveying a real sense of the college town's time, place, and faith. Yet there was in the senior colleague's final comments on the school's struggle with its religious identity a note of caution — something about the tension between being a college that wanted to preserve its ties to its founding tradition yet embrace the spirit of ecumenical Christian faith. The new colleague must have looked rattled; the senior colleague asked whether there was something the matter.

"I came to Faith with an understanding that there is a possibility, a good possibility, of a permanent appointment in Religion. That the school is embracing the part of its mission that it describes as an ecumenical Christian college by inviting a Catholic to serve in its religion department. But I detect a note of caution in your tone of voice. . . ."

"Uh . . . yes, of course we anticipate an opening or two in the coming year or so. The department wants to open up. After all, there is Chaz who teaches world religions. And Ellen is a Baptist. Of course, there is the matter of fit."

"I understand fit. That's my job this year . . . to show how a Catholic teaching scholar fits at Faith. If the fit is right, okay, if it isn't, then I understand. But the conversation during the last part of the tour, as we moved through the Catholic neighborhood, seemed to be taking another direction than ecumenicity or fit."

The ensuing lull in conversation was unbearably painful for the two. "There isn't a guarantee. I mean, let's see how the year goes," said the senior colleague finally.

After a short pause, the new colleague asked, "There is more to this tour than a tour, isn't there?"

"We are so excited that you are here. Within your first month, look at what you brought us: the course on American Catholicism, your connection between the college and the Catholic diocese — we have never had a bishop come to our campus before. The retreat for Catholic students. It's wonderful. We're just struggling with our fidelity to our own tradition." The historian fidgeted and looked deliberately at his watch. "Make sure you work hard. Oh! I have got to get along to the museum for a three o'clock lecture. Let's talk more later."

After the senior colleague departed, the newcomer was left staring long and hard into the neighborhood outside of the diner. His departmental colleagues were all outstanding scholars, teachers, and citizens. They were nice people. But now he felt more a stranger than ever in that community, an outsider. Despite their genuine hospitality, the good town and college people were uncertain about the effects of a Catholic in their religion department. He felt as if he had entered a minefield in a foreign land, where he did not speak the language. Who would he go to for wisdom about whether "working hard" here would be futile? Was there a way of flourishing here while being faithful to who he was, or had the point of the tour been to indicate gently that he should start looking now for a position elsewhere next year? He wished he knew of someone outside the religion department and administration he could confide in.

Building Ownership of the Mission and Collegiality

Because mentoring programs call on institutional resources that could be used for other purposes, it is natural to ask questions like "What difference will mentoring make to our college?" and "How important is mentoring to our faculty?" These questions will come up before institutions commit themselves to inaugurating new mentoring programs; they may also come up in connection with established programs as mentoring programs compete for scarce institutional resources with other programs within their colleges and universities.

Mentoring for Mission has highlighted the many ways that a mentoring program can make a significant difference for good in the life of your college or university. Many of the outcomes of mentoring have been documented by research studies; yet for us, the outcomes of mentoring are a matter of our lived experience.

As we have noted in Chapters One and Two, the development of faculty mentoring programs over the past years in denominational schools has been one major initiative to broaden ownership of the mission and resist missional amnesia. As a church-related college meets the institutional need for its faculty to embrace the unique identity of the school in the context of mission, it enables its faculty to be not only competent and successful in their discipline but also, through ownership of the mission, to participate fully in achieving the goals of the institution. A program with a focus on Christian mission may enhance the spiritual growth of individuals as well, by creating a forum for the discussion and development of this important component of a church-related institution.

A successful mentoring program invites new faculty to become part of a community of educators who identify with the mission spirit of the institution, fostering collegiality, dialogue, and intellectual synergy among faculty. Mentoring is an invitation not only to grow and be successful as a member of the faculty but also to participate in and be nourished by the life of the community — a *collegium*. Christian liberal arts colleges should have a special stake in the quality of their community life and strive for collegiality, trust, and open dialogue. Yet, as we have noted in the introduction, faculty at Christian colleges and universities where mentoring has not been institutionalized tend to see helping new colleagues as a fine idea for which they have too little time.

> *This year's mentoring program produced a wonderful sense of collegiality, greatly helped new faculty to feel that they were truly a part of the faculty, and gave senior faculty an opportunity to renew friendships and reflect again on their own experiences as teachers.*
>
> — End-of-year report from a mentoring director

Collegiality is vital to academic life, because it implies respect and the sharing of power among colleagues. As new and long-time faculty get acquainted, they share learning experiences, discuss recent developments in education or in their profession, and learn more about one another both personally and professionally. People who take the time to know one another are more likely to engage in constructive debate when they disagree, avoiding rancor even when they have significant disagreements about priorities or methods. Mentoring relationships, which often pair a mentor and new faculty member in different departments, strengthen webs of collegiality throughout the college.

Collegiality in turn contributes to new faculty success. Faculty need to find social supports and intellectual stimulation during the entry period of teaching. Research by Robert Boice indicates that gaining acceptance of colleagues and building social supports are more important than teaching or scholarly endeavors as predictors of new faculty success.

A positive, collegial environment promotes faculty vitality and facilitates dialogue and a desire to seek mutual understanding. It is not surprising that research shows that new faculty who are mentored will have a stronger sense of commitment and allegiance to the institution (Wunsch, 17). Through dialogue and collegial relationships, new faculty will gain an understanding of institutional lore. As new faculty members become acquainted with the mission, patron saints, revered professors (both living and dead), and school traditions and their origins, they will naturally feel a sense of ownership. A mentor can be instrumental in pointing out places of significance on campus, introducing new faculty to colorful stories that figure heavily in the college lore and heritage, telling the story behind prominent paintings and murals, and helping the newcomer acquire respect for the established peculiarities and ways of thinking that make each institution different from all others (Betty Jo Simmons, 1998).

> *How is it possible for Christian colleges and universities to mature into first-rate institutions of higher learning while, at the same time, living out of the faith traditions that gave them birth? In the field of Christian higher education, no question could be more urgent.*
>
> — Richard T. Hughes, *How Christian Faith Can Sustain the Life of the Mind*, 57

Improving Faculty Retention

The issue of faculty retention has large financial implications for a college. When faculty members leave and need to be replaced, the cost of running additional searches is high. Robert Boice estimated a decade ago that it cost between $3000 and $10,000 to hire one new faculty member. There is also a drag on an institution caused by faculty members who stay at an institution even though they have become alienated, unmotivated, or bitter. The human cost for many faculty members of reconsidering a commitment to an institution is also high. Relocating, uprooting and re-rooting a family, and re-acclimating to a new institution are stressful and time-consuming. New faculty members *want* the choice that they have made to come to a particular institution to work — they do not want to relocate; they do not want to become alienated and bitter. As Boice observes, "the costs, both economic and human, of losing new hires to competitors or to unproductive and unhappy beginnings are clearly greater than those of setting up effective support programs" (Boice, 7).

Good faculty mentoring programs make both faculty members and the institution more inclined to believe they have made the right choice when issuing and signing the initial contract. With the lack of academic positions in the 1970s, 1980s, and 1990s, many departments within colleges and universities forgot how to nurture new faculty. The assumption grew that the academy would always be a "buyer's market" where new faculty would be so grateful for a position that they would stay put even if unhappy. Yet now, in many fields, new faculty may find careers outside of academia more attractive financially. With new faculty in many fields harder to find and retain, campuses need to do a better job of making academic careers more enticing and rewarding. Moreover, the best faculty members at any school are likely to be invited to consider positions at other institutions, and they are less likely to be lured away if they have developed loyalty and satisfaction where they are.

Mentoring programs can aid in faculty retention in a variety of ways. As we indicated in the last section, by helping the new faculty member come to a fuller understanding of the history, nature, and mission of the college, mentoring can strengthen a sense of pride in the institution and loyalty to the mission. Enhancing ownership and collegiality can, in turn, counter one of the most prevalent reasons for new faculty lack of satisfaction: isolation. Obviously, a person who feels isolated within a community or who fears that he will not succeed will be likelier to leave than someone who feels confident and at home.

Yet the circumstances of faculty life in the first few years tend to isolate. First-year faculty are often "protected" from one of the natural sources of community within the college — committee work. They may feel under enough pressure from their workload that they will not initiate social interaction, but instead work through lunch and late into the night. Boice's research revealed that, "As a rule, new faculty report feeling neglected, isolated, overworked, and deprived of vital support and feedback" (44). Assigned mentors, when they serve as social initiators, can prevent new faculty members from being reduced to wandering the halls of the new institution looking for people with whom to converse when they do have some free time. A mentoring community will work to minimize feelings of alienation and isolation by designating someone who will think to drop by a new faculty person's office with an invitation to have coffee or go for a walk.

A Happy Side Effect: Rejuvenating
Veteran Faculty and Building Future Leadership

Mentoring programs not only foster good faculty retention; they also provide an opportunity to rejuvenate and honor the veteran faculty members who serve as mentors through fostering intellectual synergy. Through the mentoring relationship, both the mentor and the new faculty member can develop a greater sense of purpose for their careers. This sense of purpose promotes renewal in the mentor that may catalyze growth and the release of new capabilities.

 Those who take on the role of a mentor for new faculty are representatives of a mentoring community. Being a mentor challenges the veteran faculty member to articulate more clearly the mission and what it means in everyday interaction with students and among faculty. Being chosen to mentor new faculty members is also a recognition and honoring of effective contribution to the institution and provides a unique opportunity for growth on the part of veteran faculty members. This is a way of saying to senior faculty: you are a successful teacher and your colleagues value what you have to share. You not only teach students, you are ready to teach teachers. You not only have contributed to the mission of this school, but you also teach the mission of this school in your words and actions. You know something important about this school, and you need to share it with a new generation of faculty.

 It is not surprising that a study done by Blackburn, Chapman, and Cameron shows that senior mentors benefit from being mentors, as mentoring provides many of the revitalizing functions sought by older scholars and professionals. Such a program has the potential for becoming the focal point of intentional renewal, a continuous process in

Mentoring offers the gift of regeneration too. First the mentor needs to be open to receiving the gift. . . . Sometimes the learning comes about serendipitously.

— Lois J. Zachary, *The Mentor's Guide*, 163

which a mission-centered university or college acts as a unified community in the effort to realize its goals.

Veteran faculty mentors can also serve as role models who nurture the next generation of campus leaders. Faculty who serve as mentors often hold or have held leadership positions in the college or university. These individuals have probably also served on many college committees and have a good understanding of how to get things done in the academic environment. Through the mentoring process, new faculty can attend meetings with mentors and discuss political and leadership issues. New faculty members can learn from mentors how to solve problems positively and actively instead of complaining about problems and becoming cynical about their position or the college. Veteran faculty members can provide role models for future campus leaders.

Enhancing Professional Development

Mentoring programs can also help faculty members acquire and hone skills and abilities that will help them be productive and successful members of the campus community. Research shows that junior faculty members who receive mentoring experience a smoother process in attaining promotion and tenure and retain their positions longer (Johnsrud and Atwater). The personal attention embodied in mentoring not only helps overcome the isolation that new faculty may feel but also ensures a social support network upon which they can build a firm foundation for overall success in meeting institutional expectations.

Sir Thomas More: "But Richard . . . why not be a teacher? You'd be a fine teacher. Perhaps even a great one."

Richard: "And if I was, who would know it?"

Sir Thomas: "You, your pupils, your friends, God. Not a bad public that. . . ."

— Robert Bolt, *A Man for All Seasons*, 8-9

Effective teaching is the foundation of a successful career as a college or university professor. Boice found that new faculty need help with instructional development to gain comfort in the classroom, learn to prepare syllabi, manage difficult students, figure out unsophisticated students, and develop time management strategies (51). Mentoring new faculty helps ensure that they get the help they need in acquiring requisite skills, as well as the necessary understanding of their new home institution's particular student body.

Mentoring helps new faculty develop needed time management skills and research habits. By helping faculty improve their teaching effectiveness, scholarly activity, and understanding of students, mentoring relationships also help faculty improve their feelings about themselves. The result is competent and self-confident faculty whose accomplishments can be celebrated by the school's mentoring community.

Mentoring: A Lamp That Illuminates
Other Aspects of the Institution

We have seen how mentoring can nourish conversations about the Christian missions of our institutions and extend care to new colleagues, nurturing their skill and confidence as they settle into their complex role as teacher-scholars and find their place within their new home institution. A well-designed mentoring program can permeate the ethos of an institution, making mentoring more than programmatic, as an ethic of care and collegiality becomes an integral part of how members of the community interact.

The exercise of designing a mentoring program also forces institutions to reflect deeply on questions of identity: Who are we? What are our priorities? What are our aspirations as a Christian community of teacher-scholars? Does our community have unstated and unresolved boundary issues? Executing and evaluating a mentoring program can uncover important institutional issues: Is our sense of time shaped by a Christian faith that allows for Sabbath and hospitality or by a corporate model of driving ambition? Have we practiced justice by clearly stating institutional requirements and expectations? Have we succeeded in making new faculty from underrepresented ethnic backgrounds feel genuinely at home? Have we practiced charity by doing all we can to help new colleagues meet those expectations? How much do the faculty cultures of our divisions differ, and how well do these cultures complement one another? Addressing these questions will go beyond mentoring of new faculty, but mentoring can be a source of reflection that sheds light on both the important questions to pursue and directions to explore in answering them.

One example of an important institutional issue that can be illuminated by a mentoring program is faculty recruitment, particularly as it is related to institutional mission. Many church-related colleges and universities have, in recent years, been "recruiting for mission"; that is, they have become aware that there are tendencies in general academic culture that can lead toward secularization unless intentional efforts are made to hire significant numbers of new faculty who understand and value the Christian mission of the college.

The process of creating and sustaining a faculty who own the mission of the college begins at the stage of recruitment, but the recruitment process at many schools is complicated by differing priorities at institutional and departmental levels. Teaching faculty quite naturally tend to identify with their discipline. When departmental faculty envision the best candidate for a departmental opening, they are likely to think in terms of expertise in the sub-fields that are underrepresented in the department and someone with the very best degree, from the very best school, with the very best research agenda possible. On the other hand, academic administrators are concerned about the big picture, the fit with mission values, and whether prospective faculty will be eager to work under the conditions that are typical of a religiously based private school. Administrators may be looking for faculty who have some experience in a faith-based school or someone who shows affinity with the mission of the school; they tend to think that willingness to further the mission of the university or college is a minimal prerequisite for employment. Sometimes this subject is avoided at the department level of a search because faculty members are not sure how to bring up issues of faith and spirituality in a professional context.

If departments search for candidates with only disciplinary priorities in mind, and if they do not sufficiently inform candidates about mission-related expectations, candidates are likely to be startled when asked mission-related questions by administrators or, if hired, by mission-related aspects of a new faculty mentoring program. Candidates, administrators, and faculty may all be frustrated by resulting misunderstandings and an impression that the mission of the college is "owned" only by "the administration" and a minority of the faculty. Such a situation threatens both morale and the mission of the school.

This tension may be an abiding part of life at many church-related colleges and universities. However, conversation and collaboration about the philosophy and goals of recruiting between faculty and administration can help minimize these tensions. A mentoring program can help to frame the parameters of such a dialogue. Through the mentoring experience both new faculty and mentors participate in conversations about the mission of the college and the variety of ways of contributing to it. As ownership of the mission and a sense of collegial community increase, more faculty members become conscious of the value of the candidate who meets both disciplinary priorities and institutional mission goals. A mentoring program invites new and senior faculty alike to think beyond their own disciplines. In addition, informing job candidates about the mentoring program in which they will be invited to take part if hired provides one natural way of opening a conversation on the college's mission both at the departmental and administrative levels of a search.

The help that a mentoring program can provide for faculty recruitment for mission is just one example of how mentoring can be a lamp to illuminate issues of institutional identity and mission. Such illumination can be considered an important collateral benefit of a commitment to becoming a mentoring community. Along with enhanced ownership, retention, faculty satisfaction, and professional growth, it provides an impressive bottom line for mentoring programs. However, ultimately, the best reason to mentor goes far beyond this bottom line. Christian colleges and universities should mentor new faculty because it is the right and fitting thing to do as an exercise in Christian hospitality and care for others.

BIBLIOGRAPHY

Blackburn, Robert T., David W. Chapman, and Susan W. Cameron. "Cloning in Academe: Mentoring and Academic Careers." *Research in Higher Education* 15 (1981): 315-27.

Boice, Robert. *The New Faculty Member: Supporting and Fostering Professional Development*. San Francisco: Jossey-Bass, 1992.

Bolt, Robert. *A Man for All Seasons*. New York: Vintage, 1990 (original copyright, 1960).

Gibson, Gerald W. *Good Start: A Guidebook for New Faculty in Liberal Arts Colleges*. Bolton, MA: Anker Publishing Company, Inc., 1992.

Hughes, Richard T. *How Christian Faith Can Sustain the Life of the Mind.* Grand Rapids: Eerdmans, 2001.

Johnsrud, L., and C. Atwater. *Barriers to Tenure: Faculty Cohorts 1982-88: Technical Report.* Honolulu: University of Hawaii, 1991.

Kennedy, Donald. *Academic Duty.* Cambridge, MA: Harvard University Press, 1997.

Menges, Robert L., and associates. *Faculty in New Jobs: A Guide to Settling In, Becoming Established, and Building Institutional Support.* San Francisco: Jossey-Bass, 1999.

Simmons, Betty Jo. "Mentoring: The Route to Successful College Teaching." *The Delta Kappa Gamma Bulletin* 64, no. 4 (1998): 45-50.

Wunsch, Marie A., ed. *Mentoring Revisited: Making an Impact on Individuals and Institutions.* San Francisco: Jossey-Bass, 1994.

Zachary, Lois J. *The Mentor's Guide: Facilitating Effective Learning Relationships.* San Francisco: Jossey-Bass, 2000.

Reflection Questions for Mentoring Directors

1. How would you characterize your college's or university's particular Christian mission?
2. What expectations and priorities does your institutional mission entail? How are these relevant to faculty performance and development?
3. What parts of your institution's founding tradition and history form an important story to pass on to your new faculty? How will your mentoring program convey the story?
4. What constitutes "ownership of mission" at your school? Do you want all faculty to own your mission? What differing ways are there for faculty to do this? How can your particular program effectively cultivate ownership in new faculty?
5. What skills do your new faculty need most help in developing that are crucial to being good teacher-scholars at your institution? How will the mentoring program help in the development of these skills?
6. Given the realities of your campus life and culture, what structures of schedule, location, and format will be most effective in enabling your mentoring program to fulfill its goals?
7. On most campuses, faculty members state that time is their most valuable commodity. What is there in your mentoring program that faculty will find worthy of another time commitment?
8. Will your program mentor in groups, in mentoring pairs, or will it have a mixed format? If the latter, what aspects of mentoring

will be done within groups? What will be the particular foci of one-on-one mentoring?

9. For a mentoring program to have maximum effectiveness, participants must have freedom to discuss professional problem areas. How do you plan to create safe space for disclosure for new faculty in your mentoring program?

10. What potential challenges and obstacles are you most concerned about as you execute your mentoring program? How do you anticipate meeting them?

11. What kind of support system will you need to sustain your energy and refresh your vision? How will you seek that support?

12. What qualities do mentors most need at your institution? How will you recruit people with those qualities? What might mentors need help in knowing or doing? How will mentor training and support provide what mentors most need to do their jobs well? How do you plan to achieve the right fit between mentors and new faculty?

13. What outcomes do you seek from your mentoring program? How will you evaluate the success of your program?

14. What budgetary resources will you need for your program? How will you go about getting continuing financial support for your program?

Reflection and Discussion Questions for Mentor Training

1. Do you remember a special person who helped you get started in your teaching career? Who guided you through the complexities of the tenure process?

2. Do you remember who you talked to when you were discouraged by students' lack of response or when you were elated by a great class?

3. What were your hopes and fears when you first started at this institution? What did you find most confusing about campus or community life here? What were your biggest concerns as a new faculty member?

4. Did you have mentors? In what areas were your mentors most helpful to you? What qualities do you think make for a good mentor?

5. Have you had mentors in your educational and professional career that assisted you in relating faith with your role as a teacher-scholar? Who? How?

6. How would you state your college's or university's mission? What connections do you see between this mission and the founding religious tradition of your institution? What do you know about the founding tradition of your school? What aspects of your school's church-relatedness do you see as assets for an academic institution? Are there aspects of its church-relatedness that seem to you to inhibit academic life?

7. How do you think the Christian mission of your institution

should affect the role of teacher-scholars? How do you see the relationship between the Christian tradition and the tradition of liberal arts education?

8. Why are you at this particular school? What makes you proud and grateful to be a faculty member here? What parts of the institution's history are you excited to pass on to new faculty members?

9. What hopes for your institution's future do you have? How do you view the role of mentor as contributing to those hopes and aspirations?

10. What characteristics must a mentor have to be a genuine resource for new faculty? Do you feel you have these characteristics? How can mentor training help you to become a more effective mentor?

11. What are your expectations and concerns as you become a mentor? How can mentor training help in addressing those concerns?

12. How do you seek balance and integrity in your own life under the pressure and demands of being a faculty member? How would you seek to help new faculty achieve balance and integrity?

Questions for Mentors and New Faculty to Reflect on Together

1. What are your expectations of the mentoring relationship? How do you think a mentor can help you?
2. Why are you here? What are your primary motivations for being a teacher-scholar? How did you come to be at this particular institution?
3. How much do you know about the founding tradition and history of this college or university? What do you think it would be useful to know? Are there aspects of what you think you know that you find puzzling? What are they?
4. How do you understand the role of Christian and/or denominational identity on this campus? How do you see yourself fitting into a school with this particular Christian and/or denominational identity?
5. What motivates and excites you within your discipline and as a teacher-scholar?
6. Where do you most want to grow in the coming year as a teacher? As a scholar? As a colleague? As a person? What are your long-term hopes, dreams, and goals?
7. What sources of anxiety and stress do you find in campus life at this institution? What resources do you see here for maintaining a sense of balance and integrity? How might the mentoring relationship help in this area?
8. What are your perceptions of the evaluation, accountability, and tenure/promotion systems at this institution? Are there aspects of

those systems that you find puzzling or mysterious? How can the mentoring relationship help you in being comfortable and ultimately successful as you face evaluation for promotion at this institution?

9. What do you think your students need most in order to have an effective learning environment? What challenges are you finding in the classroom? What brings you joy and a sense of excitement as you teach?

10. Do you see your teaching and your scholarship as enhancing or as competing with one another? Are there ways that your goals as a teacher and as a scholar might be more mutually enhancing?

11. What are your greatest challenges with regard to time management? What strategies might be useful in addressing those challenges?

12. How do you see yourself contributing as a servant-leader on campus, now and in the future?

Selected Topical Bibliography

WORKS ON CHRISTIAN HIGHER EDUCATION

Benne, Robert. *Quality with Soul: How Six Premier Colleges and Universities Keep Faith with Their Religious Traditions.* Grand Rapids: Eerdmans, 2001.

Bondi, Roberta L. "Spirituality and Higher Learning." *The Cresset,* June 1993, 5-12.

Burtchaell, James Tunstead. *The Dying of the Light: The Disengagement of Colleges and Universities from Their Christian Churches.* Grand Rapids: Eerdmans, 1998.

Cutter, William. "A Theology of Teaching: Confluences and Creation." *The Melton Journal: Issues and Themes in Jewish Education* 27 (Autumn 1993): 18-21.

Dockery, David S., and David P. Gushee, eds. *The Future of Christian Higher Education.* Nashville: Broadman & Holman, 1999.

Dovre, Paul J., ed. *The Future of Religious Colleges.* Grand Rapids: Eerdmans, 2002.

Gallin, A. *Negotiating Identity: Catholic Higher Education since 1960.* Notre Dame: University of Notre Dame Press, 2000.

Holmes, Arthur F. *The Idea of a Christian College.* Grand Rapids: Eerdmans, 1975, 1987.

Hughes, Richard T., and William B. Adrian, eds. *Models for Christian Higher Education.* Grand Rapids: Eerdmans, 1997.

Hughes, Richard T. *How Christian Faith Can Sustain the Life of the Mind.* Grand Rapids: Eerdmans, 2001.

John Paul II. *Ex Corde Ecclesiae.* The official document, *Constitutio Apostolica de Universitatibus Catholicis,* was published by *Libreria Editrice Vaticana* in 1990. An English version was published by *Libreria Editrice Vaticana* and distributed by the Sacred Congregation for Catholic Education. It also appears in *Origins* 20, no. 17 (October 4, 1990): 265-76.

Knoerle, Jeanne, S.P. "The Love of Learning and the Desire for God." *The Cresset,* June/July 1997, 15-21.

Marsden, George M. *The Outrageous Idea of Christian Scholarship.* New York: Oxford University Press, 1997.

Newman, John Henry Cardinal. *The Idea of a University.* New York: Holt, Rinehart & Winston, 1960.

Palmer, Parker. *The Courage to Teach: Exploring the Inner Landscape of a Teacher's Life.* San Francisco: Jossey-Bass, 1998.

Palmer, Parker. *Let Your Life Speak.* San Francisco: Jossey-Bass, 2000.

Simmons, Ernest L. *Lutheran Higher Education: An Introduction for Faculty.* Minneapolis: Augsburg Fortress Press, 1998.

Sloan, Douglas. *Faith and Knowledge: Mainline Protestantism and American Higher Education.* Louisville: Westminster/John Knox Press, 1994.

Wilcox, J., and I. King, eds. *Enhancing Religious Identity: Best Practices from Catholic Campuses.* Washington: Georgetown University Press, 2000.

WORKS ON MENTORING

Blackburn, Robert T., David W. Chapman, and Susan W. Cameron. "Cloning in Academe: Mentoring and Academic Careers." *Research in Higher Education* 15 (1981): 315-27.

Boice, Robert. *The New Faculty Member: Supporting and Fostering Professional Development.* San Francisco: Jossey-Bass, 1992.

Collins, Nancy W. *Professional Women and Their Mentors: A Practical Guide to Mentoring for the Woman Who Wants to Get Ahead.* Englewood Cliffs, NJ: Prentice Hall, 1983.

Cunningham, Shelly. "The Nature of Workplace Mentoring Relationships among Faculty Members in Christian Higher Education." *Journal of Higher Education* 70, no. 4 (1999): 441-64.

Daloz, Laurent A. *Mentor: Guiding the Journey of Adult Learners.* San Francisco: Jossey-Bass, 1999.

English, Leona M. *Mentoring in Religious Education.* Birmingham, AL: Religious Education Press, 1998.

Gibson, Gerald W. *Good Start: A Guidebook for New Faculty in Liberal Arts Colleges.* Bolton, MA: Anker Publishing Company, Inc., 1992.

Knox, Pamela L., and Thomas V. McGovern. "Mentoring Women in Academia." *Teaching of Psychology* 15, no. 1 (1988): 39-41.

Menges, Robert L., and associates. *Faculty in New Jobs: A Guide to Settling In, Becoming Established, and Building Institutional Support.* San Francisco: Jossey-Bass, 1999.

Murray, Margo. *Beyond the Myths and Magic of Mentoring: How to Facilitate an Effective Mentoring Program.* San Francisco: HarperCollins, 1991.

Parks, Sharon Daloz. *Big Questions, Worthy Dreams: Mentoring Young Adults in Their Search for Meaning, Purpose, and Faith.* San Francisco: Jossey-Bass, 2000.

Schoenfeld, A. Clay, and Robert Magnan. *Mentor in a Manual: Climbing the Academic Ladder to Tenure.* Madison, WI: Magna Publications, 1992.

Schuster, Jack H., Daniel W. Wheeler, and associates. *Enhancing Faculty Careers: Strategies for Development and Renewal.* San Francisco: Jossey-Bass, 1990.

Wunsch, Marie A., ed. *Mentoring Revisited: Making an Impact on Individuals and Institutions.* San Francisco: Jossey-Bass, 1994.

Zachary, Lois J. *The Mentor's Guide: Facilitating Effective Learning Relationships.* San Francisco: Jossey-Bass, 2000.

Zeldin, Michael, and Sara S. Lee. *Touching the Future: Mentoring and the Jewish Professional.* Los Angeles: Rhea Hirsch School of Education, Hebrew Union College-Jewish Institute of Religion, 1995.

WORKS ON THE NATURE OF THE ACADEMY

Bennett, John B. *Collegial Professionalism: The Academy, Individualism, and the Common Good.* Phoenix: Oryx Press, 1998.

Boyer, Ernest L. *Scholarship Reconsidered: Priorities for the Professorate.* Lawrenceville, NJ: Carnegie Foundation for the Advancement of Teaching, 1990.

Carnegie Foundation for the Advancement of Teaching. "Are Liberal Arts Colleges Really Different?" *Change* (March/April 1990), 42-44.

Marsden, George. *The Soul of the American University: From Protestant Establishment to Established Nonbelief.* New York: Oxford University Press, 1994.

Schwehn, Mark R. *Exiles from Eden: Religion and the Academic Vocation in America.* New York: Oxford University Press, 1993.

Tompkins, Jane. *A Life in School: What the Teacher Learned.* Reading, MA: Addison-Wesley, 1996.

Willimon, William H., and Thomas H. Naylor. *The Abandoned Generation: Rethinking Higher Education.* Grand Rapids: Eerdmans, 1995.

Contributors

CAROLINE J. SIMON (lead author) is professor of philosophy at Hope College in Holland, Michigan. She specializes in ethics, with an emphasis on the use of literature in moral reflection. She is the author of *The Disciplined Heart: Love, Destiny and Imagination,* and has published many articles on subjects that include moral knowledge, virtue ethics, and sexuality. She has served on the editorial boards of two journals that relate the Christian faith to the intellectual life. She directed the Lilly Mentoring Initiative, the series of consultations out of which this book grew.

LAURA BLOXHAM is a professor of English at Whitworth College in Spokane, Washington, where for four years she served as acting associate dean and then director of faculty development. Her specialty is British Romantic poetry, but she also teaches Southern literature, religious themes in modern literature, and a number of courses in the nineteenth and twentieth centuries, British, American, and world literatures. She has published on Alice Walker and reviews books for a variety of publications, especially those with theological orientations. In 1988 she was named CASE Professor of the Year for the state of Washington.

DENISE DOYLE is Vice President for Academic and Student Affairs at the University of the Incarnate Word in San Antonio, Texas. She holds a Ph.D. and J.C.D. in Canon Law from St. Paul University in Ottawa, Canada. She has served at Incarnate Word in a variety of capacities since

1988, is a member of the Department of Religious Studies, and has been active in faculty governance. She chaired the Justice and Peace graduate program and the Pastoral Institute. She founded an adult degree completion program and was the first dean of the School of Extended Studies.

MEL HAILEY is chair and professor of political science at Abilene Christian University in Abilene, Texas. He specializes in political theory with a particular interest in religion and politics. He is the co-author of *Ministers at the Millennium,* and he has served as an officer and executive board member of Christians in Political Science. Active in his local community, he served as a founding board member and president of Abilene Habitat for Humanity, as a board member of Meals on Wheels, and as chair of the board of directors of the Noah Project, a shelter for victims of family violence.

JANE HOKANSON HAWKS is an associate professor of nursing at Midland Lutheran College, Fremont, Nebraska. She is the editor of *Urologic Nursing* and co-authored a medical-surgical nursing textbook published in 2001, her third book publication. Dr. Hawks has also authored numerous articles and textbook chapters and provided presentations related to empowering teaching strategies, empowerment, mentoring, power, alcoholism in families, and urologic and gastrointestinal problems. She serves on the mentoring steering committee and has been a co-coordinator of the Midland Lutheran mentoring program for six years.

KATHLEEN LIGHT is an associate professor of nursing and Dean of the School of Nursing and Health Professions at University of the Incarnate Word in San Antonio, Texas. She has taught child health nursing, management and leadership, nursing ethics, and health promotion. Her publications include articles related to health promotion, wellness, nursing ethics, and nursing history. Dr. Light has directed the faculty mentoring program at University of the Incarnate Word for the past three years.

DOMINIC P. SCIBILIA is a member of the religion faculty at St. Peter's Preparatory School in New Jersey. He has published essays and articles on historical theology, especially regarding lay and clerical Catholic labor figures in the United States, and on advancing a sacramental pedagogy. Since 1995 he has been affiliated with the Rhodes Consultation on the Future of Church-Related Colleges. Dr. Scibilia contributed a chapter on teaching college theology for *Professing in the Postmodern Academy.*

ERNEST SIMMONS is a professor of religion and director of the Dovre Center for Faith and Learning at Concordia College, Moorhead, Minnesota. An ordained ELCA pastor who served several congregations before joining the faculty of Concordia, his publications include articles on the theology of Martin Luther, issues in science and religion, and the relation of faith and learning in higher education. He is a recipient of several Templeton Foundation awards for his coursework and writing in science and religion. He is author of the book *Lutheran Higher Education* and is currently Book Review Editor for the journal *Dialog.*